GAIN YOUR FINANCIAL FREEDOM
with the 1% FORMULA

Deepak Mullick has a 27-year-long career in the investments industry. This includes his stint with HDFC Mutual Fund as their business head for North, South and East India during different parts of his tenure. After gaining his own financial freedom at the age of 45, Deepak does what he loves—travelling and spending time with his family. Following his passion, he is currently a professional investment practitioner, helping his clients achieve their financial freedom. He can be reached through his website (www.simplymutual.com) and over email (info@simplymutual.com). His financial freedom community on Facebook is available at https://www.facebook.com/ simplymutual.

GAIN YOUR FINANCIAL FREEDOM
with the 1% FORMULA

DEEPAK MULLICK

Best Wishes for your financial freedom!

Published by
Rupa Publications India Pvt. Ltd 2023
7/16, Ansari Road, Daryaganj
New Delhi 110002

Sales centres:
Bengaluru Chennai
Hyderabad Jaipur Kathmandu
Kolkata Mumbai Prayagraj

Copyright © Deepak Mullick 2023

The views and opinions expressed in this book are
the author's own and the facts are as reported by him
which have been verified to the extent possible,
and the publishers are not in any way liable for the same.

All rights reserved.
No part of this publication may be reproduced, transmitted,
or stored in a retrieval system, in any form or by any means,
electronic, mechanical, photocopying, recording or otherwise,
without the prior permission of the publisher.

P-ISBN: 978-93-5702-656-7
E-ISBN: 978-93-5702-693-2

First impression 2023

10 9 8 7 6 5 4 3 2 1

The moral right of the author has been asserted.

Printed in India

This book is sold subject to the condition that it shall not,
by way of trade or otherwise, be lent, resold, hired out, or otherwise
circulated, without the publisher's prior consent, in any form of binding
or cover other than that in which it is published.

In the loving memory of my mother

Contents

Disclaimer ix

1. How I Gained My Freedom at 45 — 1
2. You Don't Need to Be a Finance Whiz Kid to Be a Financial Success — 8
3. Decoding the Share Market — 28
4. The Money Mindset — 59
5. Roti, Kapda and 2BHK — 80
6. The 1 per cent Formula to Financial Freedom — 99
7. Making the 1 per cent Formula Work for Your Unique Needs — 123
8. Success Stories of the 1 per cent Formula — 147
9. A Word of Caution — 166
10. The 10 Commandments of Wealth Building — 171

A Letter to the Individual Investor 184
Acknowledgements 186

Disclaimer

This book is about investing in equity through mutual funds (MFs). Before you read further, the author would like you to keep a few things in mind.

Mutual fund investments are subject to market risks, so you should read all the scheme-related documents carefully. The Net Asset Value (NAV) of the schemes may go up or down depending upon the factors and forces affecting the securities market, including the fluctuations in the interest rates. The past performance of the MFs is not necessarily indicative of the future performance of these schemes. As an investor, you should review the offer document carefully and obtain expert professional advice with regard to specific legal, tax and financial implications of the investment/participation in the scheme.

While all efforts have been taken to make this book as factual as possible, you are requested to please refer to the print versions and notified Gazette copies of Acts/Rules/Regulations for authentic version or for use before any authority. The author would not be held responsible for any loss to any person or entity caused by any shortcomings, defects or inaccuracies that have, inadvertently or otherwise, crept in this book.

This book is for general information only and does not have regard to specific investment objectives, financial situation and the particular needs of any specific person who may receive this information. This book provides general information on performance; financial planning and/or comparisons are only for illustration purposes. The data/information/framework, including the 1 per cent formula, used/disclosed in this book is only for information purposes and does not guarantee or indicate any returns. Investments in MFs and secondary markets inherently involve risks, and you should consult your legal, tax and financial advisors before investing.

You should also understand that any and all references to indices, sectors, securities, schemes, et al. in the book are for illustration purposes alone and should not be considered as recommendation(s). As the reader of this information, you should understand that statements made herein regarding future prospects may not be realized or achieved. The distribution of this book in certain jurisdictions may be restricted or totally prohibited, and, accordingly, anyone who comes into possession of this book is required to inform themselves about, and to observe, any such restrictions.

All the stories of people in the book are inspired by true events but the names and situations have been changed to protect identities. All stories from the author's life and experiences have been depicted truthfully.

1

How I Gained My Freedom at 45

On a warm summer evening in 1947, my grandparents packed their bags and left their life behind. *Freedom.* That was the chant in the air. History was being created as the British left a partitioned India behind. For millions of people, this meant leaving behind everything they owned—their life's work and savings, the security and comfort of their homes—and moving to unknown lands with an uncertain future. My grandparents, too, made their way from Dera Ismail Khan in the Khyber Pakhtunkhwa province of what is now Pakistan to Lucknow, Uttar Pradesh.

I grew up hearing the stories of their lives. In the evenings, when we all sat together in the courtyard of my grandparents' house, they would get nostalgic. My grandmother would tell us about our culture, our food, the traditions, all the wealth we had, the land we owned back then, and how we earned our surname 'Mullick'—a title given to big landlords. Even as a child, I could hear the longing in her voice as well as a note of bitterness at being uprooted. When I write this now from the comfort of my home, I can't even imagine what they must have gone through. They had moved with just a few suitcases, hurriedly packed; and had travelled hundreds of miles in search of a new place to settle in an environment of extreme hostility. They must have experienced immense stress and anxiety of not knowing where they were headed as well as despondency of having to start living from scratch.

But start again, they did! And they did it quite successfully too.

Why am I telling you this? What does a story about uprooting and migration have to do with a book on wealth building?

Well, in this story, there is a lesson—that life is unpredictable, that ups and downs will happen, that, sometimes, everything you take for granted will be disrupted. But it is important to not lose your wits. Financial success is all about thinking of the long term. As the poster boy for long-term investing, Warren Buffett said, 'Successful Investing takes time, discipline and patience.'[1]

I'll add to that and say wealth building is also about optimism. I consider myself an eternal optimist. It's in my DNA!

I learnt important life lessons—resilience, optimism and street-smartness—from my parents, grandparents and my alma mater *La Martiniere*, which have helped me immensely on my path to financial freedom.

After I finished my schooling, I had the easy option to join the family business. But it wasn't something that interested me. I wanted to look at work as something that would help me live the life I desired, and I am very unapologetic about it. I am a firm believer that you work to live and not live to work. Have you ever thought about it?

---

[1] Dzombak, Dan, 'How to Become Rich, and 24 Other Insights from Warren Buffett', *Time*, https://tinyurl.com/tr8m6phk. Accessed on 19 September 2023.

What would you do if you had all the money you needed to live a comfortable life? Would you still pursue the job you currently have? Would you go after something that you are truly passionate about? Would you give and contribute to the world? Would you spend time travelling the world, experiencing new things and gaining different perspectives?

Most of us spend a lot of time in the lower two stages of Maslow's hierarchy of needs (Figure 1). We struggle to make enough money to pay for our basic needs of food, clothing and shelter. We compromise on building meaningful relationships and on finding our true potential often because that raise or that promotion is so much more important. Well, I didn't want to live all my life with some golden handcuffs.

So, my aim was to find a career path that would help me realize my retirement goals (yes, I was thinking of retirement when I was 20!) by the time I turned 45—a highly ambitious goal given India's economic situation, then. However, in a series of seemingly unconnected events, I found my calling.

In the early 1990s, when I was considering my career choices, the financial services sector was abuzz with activity. India was undergoing an economic transformation. Raising itself out of a bottomless pit of foreign aid, India formulated economic liberalization policies that aimed to make it an emerging superpower in just two decades. Companies were coming up with initial public offerings (IPOs) every other day, and there was a huge demand for finance talent. Later, this timeframe would also be known as the 'IPO scam' period. Amidst this turmoil, I graduated with an MBA degree and a campus placement at a financial services company that gave me a take-home salary of about ₹5,000 a month.

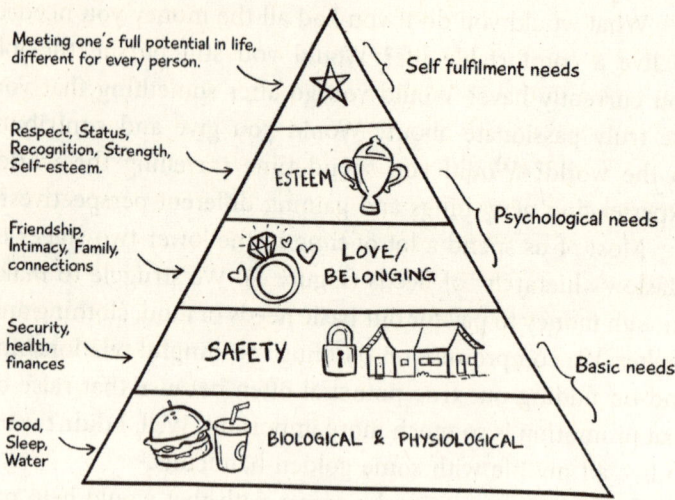

Figure 1: Maslow's Hierarchy of Needs

From a starting point of ₹5,000 per month to a sizable corpus of a few crores, I have come a long way, retiring at 45 as I had envisioned. I have lived well. I have indulged in my passions and in things that interest my family and me. We have travelled extensively and experienced the world closely. From whisky trails to the Northern Lights, we have made our way to 29 countries across five continents.

This financial freedom has been a journey of considerable learning. First, I found a god sent friend, philosopher and guide with whom I have had the privilege of working for two decades. And then, for over three decades, I had the opportunity to witness the rapid evolution of the country's economic constituents—the businesses, the consumers, the regulatory environment, government policy, the markets and the ever-changing global scene. I have figured out what works and what doesn't. I have learnt to tame the volatility and invest in a way that sustains my lifestyle choices while building my corpus of funds. I have distilled this learning into this book and created the *1 per cent formula to gain financial freedom*.

The idea of this book came from my experiences of sharing my technique with friends and family members who wanted to quit the rat race and pursue other life goals and passions. And most of them have benefitted by following my technique.

I realized that there is an overload of irrelevant information, no dearth of wealth-destruction products and an acute scarcity of good advice in the investments industry. *Gain Your Financial Freedom* is my passionate attempt to bring about an easier understanding of the opportunities and to simplify long-term wealth creation.

This book is written as an equity-investing guide for those who are keen to make their money work for them. It is meant for people in their 20s and 30s who are looking to retire by 45, those who have 7–10 years before they want to retire and those who want an easy-to-understand insight into how investing works. This book is your ticket to long-term wealth creation and living comfortably off that wealth without giving in to stress, anxiety or overwork.

In this book, I will tell you the secrets to financial success. I will share stories of people who have seen the light and changed their investing behaviours for enormous gains. I will help you build good investing habits and make informed investment choices. I will explain the different assets you invest money in—both physical and financial—and why some of them are actually eroding your wealth. While I'll touch upon these, I will not cover the entire umbrella of financial planning and management in great detail, and there is a reason for that. I believe that if you understand equities the right way and work with the 1 per cent formula, you will not need other kinds of investment vehicles as much.

In my 25 years of experience in the financial sector, I have gained a fair idea of the practices in the banking industry, the insurance industry and the quality of the advisory businesses across categories. I have worked with several financial planners, attended many workshops and dived deep into the subject of financial and investment planning. I've looked at all asset classes—real estate, gold, debt, equity, foreign equity, etc.—from the lens of factors such as returns adjusting for risks, returns adjusting for inflation and taxes, liquidity, volatility, convenience and costs of investing. I've realized that equity MF (EMF) is where the best balance can be achieved. In fact, I've been able to pull out of my term life insurance policies because of the corpus I have built through EMF investments!

And so, this book will deal in investing via equity only, and more explicitly, investing in equity through MFs. For the purpose of this book, I am also considering hybrid MFs with over 65 per cent investments in equity as EMFs.

By reading this book, you will:

1. get a better understanding of the opportunity India offers, how long will it remain and how exactly to benefit from it
2. get the right perspective on share markets, understand emotional hurdles and mistakes on the way to financial freedom and gain insights on how to benefit from the markets
3. learn a simple equity-based technique to build wealth and to create your own 'salary–pension' stream for retirement

Like every great adventure, this book is a start. And as you read it, I'd like to give a word of caution. This book focusses on financial resilience. That means periods of no-gain, or even loss, that you sit through for long-term returns. This book is *not* about quick fixes or immediate gains. If thinking long-term does not appeal to you, then this book is not for you.

That said, in the coming pages, there is a wealth of knowledge and tried and tested methods that work. I hope you find them as useful as I have and apply them to achieve your financial freedom.

2
You Don't Need to Be a Finance Whiz Kid to Be a Financial Success

'Most people understand complexity as intelligence; if they make themselves difficult, they are supposed to be intelligent. Making a simple thing difficult is not intelligence. Making a very complex thing simple is intelligence!'

—Sadhguru Jaggi Vasudev

India Opportunity

Have you ever wondered how people get rich? Let me give you a hint.

Who are the richest people on this planet?

The year-end rankings on the Forbes website for 2022[1] listed the top 10 as:

1. Elon Musk of Tesla, with his personal wealth valued at $219B
2. Jeff Bezos of Amazon at $171B
3. Bernard Arnault of Louis Vuitton Moët Hennessy at $158B
4. Bill Gates of Microsoft at $129B
5. Warren Buffett of Berkshire Hathaway at $118B
6. Larry Page of Google at $111B
7. Sergey Brin of Google at $107B
8. Larry Ellison of Oracle at $106B
9. Steve Ballmer of Microsoft at $91.4B
10. Mukesh Ambani of Reliance at $90.7B

What's the one thing that is common among all these people? They own a large number of shares of successful business enterprises—they own equities!

INDIA: THE GOLDEN GOOSE OF OPPORTUNITY FOR EVERYONE

The richest businessmen have created their wealth through the creation of successful business enterprises. This success happened when:

---

[1]'Forbes World's Billionaires List 2022: The Top 200', *Forbes*, 5 April 2022, https://tinyurl.com/3rycbuvp. Accessed on 19 September 2023.

- their respective countries went through a sustained cycle of growth in economic activity, and
- demand for goods and services was strong, and their companies catered to that demand and generated profits over long periods of time.

In the process, not only did they create a whole lot of personal wealth but also enhanced the riches of all the stakeholders who partnered in their business by buying their shares. One of the best examples of such shareholders is also on the list—Warren Buffett. While all others on the list have built business empires from the bottom up, he made his riches from his expertise in identifying and investing in successful companies built by others.

A combination of factors is conducive for an economy to thrive: political stability, technological advances, infrastructure expansion, self-sufficiency in agriculture, high literacy, increasing affordability of consumers, a strong defence, general law and order and the most important one—attractive demographics.

The working age, as defined by the Organization for Economic Cooperation and Development (OECD), lies between 15 and 64 years.[2] Economists have, for long, analysed the attractiveness of economies as a percentage of the population in the working age. A predominantly young, working-age population can be the biggest asset to an economy. This is the age bracket when people are their most productive. They not only produce more goods and services but also consume more, and that is really good for the economy.

---

[2] 'Working Age Population', *OECD*, https://tinyurl.com/54m5yn5m. Accessed on 15 September 2023.

Young Population Boosts the Economy

All the (now) developed nations—Japan, the United Kingdom (UK), France, Italy, Germany and the United States of America (USA)—have had their periods of highest economic growth rates correspond to the peaks in their working-age population. These were the years that eventually made them economic superpowers! This phenomenon is now working in India's favour. Let me elaborate on how this happens through my own example.

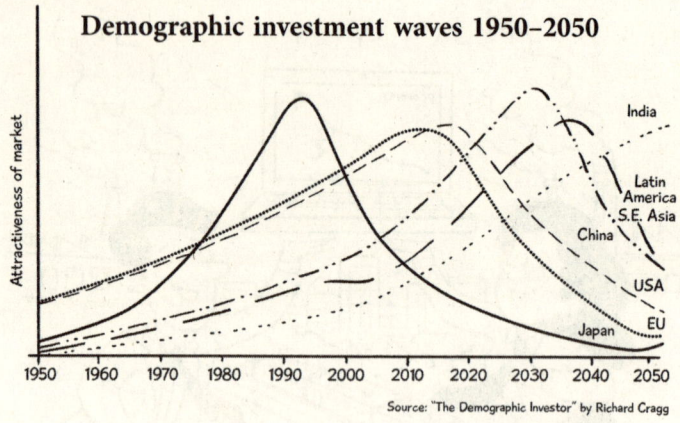

Figure 2: Demographic investment waves 1950–2050

Source: Cragg, Richard, *Demographic Investor*, Financial Times/Prentice Hall, 1998.

In 1996, when I completed my MBA and got a job, I had to leave my joint-family home in Lucknow and move to where the job took me—Delhi. This move meant that I had to set up a separate residence altogether—rent a house, buy some furniture, kitchen utensils, a refrigerator and a few other household items to keep my bachelor life comfortable. Later, when I got married, a mini-economic boom started to happen. My wife and I were working in large, private-sector organizations in the telecom and financial services industries (contributing to the supply side in these sectors), respectively.

Leveraging our combined salaries, we moved to a bigger rented house (creating demand for real estate), bought more furnishings and kitchenware, a bigger refrigerator, a television, a music system, a washing machine, water heaters and air-conditioners (creating demand for consumer durables). We bought a two-wheeler and, a few years later, a car (creating demand for the auto sector). Over the years, we hired temporary services from cooks, domestic workers, carpenters, drivers and plumbers (creating employment). We spent money on eating out, travelling (creating demand for the hospitality sector) and other areas of discretionary spending. When we had children, our economic unit started contributing to childcare, education and the investments industry.

Now just imagine: 50 per cent of our 141-crore population can go through this phenomenon in the next three decades. Yes, 50 per cent of our population is below the age of 28 today. This means that there will be a regular induction of individuals into the working-age group. Across the income strata, as children grow up and get access to more opportunities—moving out of poverty or away from small towns and villages to urban areas in pursuit of careers (as I did)—joint economic units will birth more economic units, sequentially increasing demand for goods and services at all levels of income. Current estimates say that every minute, 30 people are making such a move in India![3]

In the year 2021, India had more than 950 million of its population in this age group, a close second to China, which had about 977 million. As I write this book in 2023, sometime in the next few months, India will overtake China to have the largest working-age population across the globe. And that means more economic growth and thriving businesses with growing profits for the next three decades.

---

[3] JPIN Global, 'Treasury Leadership Forum 2023 Deepak Bagla', *YouTube*, 23 February 2023, https://tinyurl.com/4f6jmhyp. Accessed on 11 September 2023.

Creation of new economic units

Even for the existing consumer base, the penetration of goods and services in Indian households is currently very low compared to other emerging markets (EMs) (see Table 1). After the lull of the pandemic, there is a pent-up demand that will see expression in the coming few years.

Table 1
Consumer goods penetration relative to other EMs

Country	Refrigeration	Home Laundry	Room AC	Two-Wheelers	Four-Wheelers
India	37%	15.80%	5.50%	54.60%	9.70%
China	95%	91.90%	109.30%	44.90%	51.70%
Brazil	98.50%	66.90%	NA	26.40%	49.40%

Source: HDFC MF Yearbook 2021, https://tinyurl.com/ms29h854. Accessed on 19 September 2023.

There are immense opportunities for businesses to bridge the gaps in the high under-penetration of goods and services and massive unmet demand for infrastructure (roads, bridges, ports, airports and public transport) in India, especially in rural and remote areas.

As affluence grows across income segments of Indian households, it creates a massive demand, providing a boost to almost every sector. As shown in Figure 3, India is fast reducing its low-income, dependent-on-government-support households and rapidly increasing the number of contributors to its economic growth. Around the end of this decade, it is estimated that one in every two households will be in the high or upper middle income household category, and India

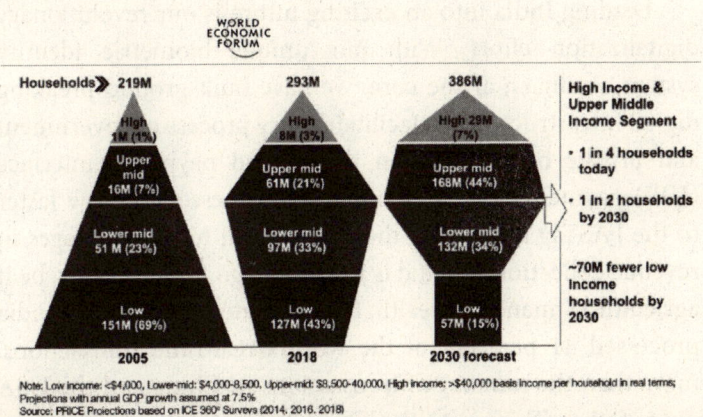

Figure 3: Evolution of household-income profile in India

Source: Cited in Ohja, Nikhil Prasad and Radhika Sridharan, 'How India's New Consumers can Contribute to a $6 Trillion Opportunity', *World Economic Forum*, 1 October 2019, https://tinyurl.com/2f64hxyk. Accessed on 11 September 2023.

would have pushed 70 million households out of poverty. With smartphone users estimated to cross a billion in the next few years, the Indian consumers will create one of the largest markets to be wooed by businesses from across the globe.[4]

If you look back at the list of the wealthiest people, consumer-oriented business owners like Louis Vuitton and Amazon feature prominently. The bigwigs of developed nations rode the consumption wave to make their money, and now it's time for India.

According to a Morgan Stanley report, the global trends of demographics, digitalization, multi-polarization and decarbonization are favouring the new India and enabling it to emerge as one of the world's largest hubs for both manufacturing and services.[5]

Leading India into an exciting future is our revolutionary digitalization effort. With our unique biometric identity system, Aadhaar, at the core, we have built ground-breaking digital infrastructures to facilitate every process of government and private business. From the unified payments interface (UPI) payments system facilitating businesses to grow faster to the FASTag facilitating the government to plug leakages in revenue collections, digital is the way to go for all sectors, be it agriculture, finance or health. It is estimated that in 2021, India processed 41 per cent of the world's real-time transactions, more than the number of transactions in China and the USA put together. This is just the beginning, and more innovations and disruptions in the field of digitalization are underway.

---

[4]'India to Have 1 Billion Smartphone Users by 2026: Deloitte Report', *Business Standard*, 22 February 2022, https://tinyurl.com/ap6e3uwe. Accessed on 19 September 2023.

[5]*Why This Is India's Decade*, Morgan Stanley Bluepapers, 31 October 2022.

On the decarbonization front as well, India is making big strides. By signing the Paris Agreement and committing to a net-zero-emissions status by 2070, we are transitioning towards self-reliance. India's projected high growth means higher energy needs, and plans are underway to meet these needs with indigenously manufactured renewable sources. Solar energy is a hugely untapped source as approximately 80 per cent of our lands get sunlight 80 per cent of the time. Among others, hydrogen seems to be another resource currently being researched by India extensively to tap into, and thereby reduce its dependence on imported fuel sources.

The government policies to facilitate India's growth are also nothing short of path-breaking. Across the country, we now see a growth spurt, owing to 100 per cent rural electrification,[6] increasing smartphone connectivity, etc., facilitated by government reforms such as the Jan Dhan Yojana, Digital India, Startup India and Pradhan Mantri Awas Yojana. There are initiatives planned to make India a bigger tourist destination, a wellness destination and a hub of creating film content.

Initiatives like Make in India and Ease of Doing Business initiatives have brought in unprecedented amounts of foreign investments across sectors and in new projects spread over the length and breadth of the country. Encouraging policies for entrepreneurs has made India, in 2022, the number one country in creation of new start-ups, number two in overall number of start-ups and number three in overall number of unicorns.[7] There is a targeted effort to create a conducive

---

[6] '100% Village Electrification Achieved in India', *Press Information Bureau*, 27 July 2022, https://tinyurl.com/yp3eame8. Accessed on 19 September 2023.
[7] JPIN Global, 'Treasury Leadership Forum 2023 Deepak Bagla', *YouTube,* 23 February 2023, https://tinyurl.com/4f6jmhyp. Accessed on 11 September 2023.

environment for investments, thereby generating jobs that will translate into wages and, in turn, increase consumption to eventually lead to a virtuous cycle of growth.

In addition, the pandemic has made remote working acceptable. It's anticipated that a large portion of services jobs will be moving to India. And these will not be limited to the traditional informational technology (IT) or business process outsourcing (BPO) jobs, but will also cover accounting, taxation, human resources (HR), payroll, engineering support, etc.

The manufacturing industry is booming too. As the economic world becomes multipolar, the dominant positions of China as a manufacturing hub and the USA as a consumption hub are shifting to other economies, and India is primed to receive a major chunk of the production investment. It is already an established global technology and pharmaceutical hub. After witnessing the supply chain disruptions during Covid-19, the world is looking to reduce its dependence on a single country and keenly looking towards India to diversify production and supply chains. The Indian government is leaving no stone unturned in making this shift happen. The launch of the Production-Linked Incentive (PLI) schemes and the announcement of lower taxes for setting up new manufacturing facilities have the sector all fired up.

My mentor Prashant Jain, an iconic fund manager, said in a recent interview, 'India's economic growth prospects are the best I have seen in my three decades' career.'[8] His reasons echo the sentiments of the Morgan Stanley report foreseeing a

---

[8]Forbes India, 'Prashant Jain's Golden Rules of Investing for Market-Beating Returns | Part 2', *YouTube*, 25 January 2023, https://tinyurl.com/4zbtkc2p. Accessed on 11 September 2023.

growing share in both services and manufacturing—a unique circumstance for the first time in modern history for any country. He predicts that India's real growth rate, which was averaging 6 per cent over the last 20 years, could move up to 7 or 8 per cent for the next few decades.

After growing bigger than the economies of Russia, Italy, Brazil, France and the UK in the last decade, India is slated to pull ahead of Germany and Japan as well in the current decade. It is on track to become the third largest economy by 2031, with the gross domestic product (GDP) crossing $7.5 trillion, doubling in size from the current levels. Alongside this growth, India's equity market capitalization will also grow three times to reach $10 trillion.

So, there is a lot happening on the economic front—enough to fill another book.

THE OPPORTUNITY IS YOURS TO TAKE

When an economy like India does well, it is a reflection of the businesses running in the country doing well. If you want to build wealth to retire early and pursue your passions, there are only two ways to go about it:

1. Start a business and make it successful
2. Become a part-owner in an existing successful business

The first option is great but also difficult. Not everyone has the acumen or diligence to make a business successful. What's more, you may not even *want* to run a business and deal with its daily operations! Starting a business comes with its own risks. Many new businesses end up failing and shut their doors before they become profitable.

On the other hand, when you become a part-owner of a business, you reap the dividends of their growth without lifting a finger. It's very easy to become a part-owner of an already successful business—all you need to do is buy their shares. Wisely!

How to Build Wealth?

If you had started investing in the share market in 1979, by 2023, your investment (tied to the Sensex) would have grown at 16 per cent compounded annualized growth rate (CAGR).[9]

---

[9]CAGR calculation for the Sensex, which was at 100 in March 1979 and 58,992 in March 2023

If you picked up some well-managed, equity-oriented schemes from private-sector MFs in 1993–94, your returns could have been about 17–19 per cent CAGR.[10]

Investments in fixed deposits (FDs) or gold in the same timeframe would have given you somewhere around 8–9 per cent CAGR, depending on what you chose.[11]

However, if you picked up real estate in the 2000s, it's quite likely that it's given you negative returns since the global financial crisis in 2008.

Clearly, participating in the growth of Indian enterprise has been very remunerative in the last three decades.

Successful Indian businessmen are already climbing the ladder to be among the world's richest. The 2022 Forbes list of top 10 richest Indians[12] includes:

1. Mukesh Ambani of Reliance at $90.7B
2. Gautam Adani of Adani Group at $90B
3. Shiv Nadar of HCL at $28.7B
4. Cyrus Poonawalla of Serum Institute at $24.3B
5. Radhakishan Damani of DMart at $20B
6. Lakshmi Mittal of ArcelorMittal at $17.9B
7. Savitri Jindal of Jindal Group at $17.7B
8. Kumar Birla of Aditya Birla Group at $16.5B
9. Dilip Shanghvi of Sun Pharma at $15.6B
10. Uday Kotak of Kotak Bank at $14.3B

---

[10] Calculated on the basis of MF factsheets (for details, see 'Beating inflation with the 1 per cent formula', Chapter 6).

[11] Calculated on the basis of data available from Bloomberg, *RBI Handbook of Statistics on Indian Economy*, National Savings Institute and State Bank of India (for details, see 'Asset class comparison', Chapter 5).

[12] Karmali, Naazneen, 'India's 10 Richest Billionaires 2022', *Forbes*, 5 April 2022, https://tinyurl.com/2f568r3u. Accessed on 19 September 2023.

In a few more years, the Damanis and Nadars of India could be neck and neck with their counterparts in Forbes 2022 list on top 10 wealthiest people and might even surpass them. We could have our very own Warren Buffett too!

Those who understand the opportunity India is sitting on, from their own experience elsewhere, have already started to raise their stakes. Foreign institutional investors (FIIs), including several pension funds and foreign MFs, recognized this potential and made significant investments in India as soon as it opened its doors to them in 1992. By the end of the last decade, these entities had accumulated ownership of approximately one-fourth of the shares of our listed entities, second only to the promoter holdings that stood at about 50 per cent.[13]

Domestic investors in India (individuals or institutions) have been late in recognizing this opportunity. It is only in the last seven to nine years that their holdings have risen from a meagre single-digit percentage to finally surpass the foreign investors.[14] In developed markets like the USA, domestic investors own more than half of equity markets, and given the recent developments, India is headed in that direction.

If you think you have missed the bus, don't worry—you

---

[13]Sethuraman, Sundar, 'Shareholding of FPIs in Listed Companies at Five-Year High, Shows Data', Business Standard, 9 February 2021, https://tinyurl.com/4uujvwsh. Accessed on 11 September 2023; Sethuraman, Sundar, 'FPI's December-End Shareholding in NSE-Listed Firms at 5-Year High of 23%', Business Standard, 8 February 2021, https://tinyurl.com/4prpcvmr. Accessed on 11 September 2023.

[14]Sethuraman, Sundar, 'Domestic Investor Holding in Listed Stocks Hits New High, Shows Data', *Business Standard*, 14 November 2022, https://tinyurl.com/37dnbj35. Accessed on 11 September 2023.

are not alone! The good news is that there's much more to gain in the coming decades.

This is a fantastic time to be an investor in India. In every decade[15] for the last four decades—despite political, economic, communal and technological upheavals—India's GDP has registered a nominal[16] growth rate of 12–15 per cent and real/post inflation GDP growth at 6 per cent. What this means is that industry—both manufacturing and services—have been doing phenomenally well. And this growth will continue.

The top analysts in the world are bullish on India's growth story. Goldman Sachs expects India to be the second largest economy in the world by 2045.[17]

Morgan Stanley, in its report titled 'India: Why This Is India's Decade', projects India's real GDP growth rates to average at 6.5 per cent in the next decade.[18]

'It's not India's decade, it's India's century,' says Bob Sternfels, CEO of McKinsey.[19]

'India's economic growth prospects are the best I have seen in my three decades' career,' says Prashant Jain, India's oldest fund manager.[20]

---

[15]For the purpose of this book, the decades start from 0s and end at 9s, so that 2019 is the end of last decade.
[16]Not adjusted for inflation
[17]Poddar, Tushar and Eva Yi, *India's Rising Growth Potential*, Global Economics Paper No. 152, Goldman Sachs, 22 January 2007.
[18]'India: Why This Is India's Decade', *Morgan Stanley*, https://tinyurl.com/2r8ekb2w. Accessed on 15 September 2023.
[19]'It's Not India's Decade, It's India's Century, Says McKinsey's Bob Sternfels', *The Economic Times*, 2 September 2022, https://tinyurl.com/yy8f2dey. Accessed on 19 September 2023.
[20]Forbes India, 'Prashant Jain's Golden Rules of Investing for Market-Beating Returns | Part 2', *YouTube*, 25 January 2023, https://tinyurl.com/4zbtkc2p.

'We are very bullish on India,' says EM veteran Mark Mobius.[21]

There is a consensus among global analyst firms and economic agencies that India will be the fastest growing large economy for the next couple of decades, if not more.

All indicators point to the fact that opportunities in India to create wealth will continue to exist for another 30 years, and anyone can capitalize on it. The question is, are you ready to participate in this wealth creation?

THE TIME TO START IS NOW!

When you are in your early 30s, retirement isn't something you actively think about. It's easy to defer investments for another day. But each day you choose to delay your investment decisions is where you lose money. The earlier you start investing, the better it is for your financial health and the lesser a burden on your day-to-day expenses. Let's see how that works.

Arun and Samar were two friends who got their first jobs in 1993 when they were 22. In 1994, the HDFC Balanced Advantage Fund was introduced, and Arun started a monthly systematic investment plan (SIP) of just ₹1,800 in this fund. In 2019, after 25 years, Arun's wealth creation from this fund alone amounted to ₹1 crore. On the other hand, Samar started investing in the same fund in 2009, when he was 38 years old, only when a lot of responsibilities had begun to sink in. He

---

Accessed on 11 September 2023.

[21]moneycontrol, 'Live: Mark Mobius Exclusive | Why Mobius Is Bullish On India | India View, Adani Rout & More', *YouTube*, 8 February 2023, https://tinyurl.com/yjv8teh8. Accessed on 19 September 2023.

started an SIP of ₹10,000, more than five times the amount that Arun was investing, and yet, by 2019, the wealth created in 10 years was less than ₹24 lakh—a quarter of what Arun made.

Looking at fund performance (Table 2), Samar would have had to start investing ₹42,000 per month to build the same ₹1 crore in 10 years. That's a sizable investment compared to Arun's contribution of ₹1,800 a month.

Table 2
HDFC Balanced Advantage Fund

To make a crore				
No. of years till 2019	25	20	15	10
Monthly SIP Amt (INR)	₹1,800	₹4,800	₹16,300	₹42,000
₹1,800 pm would be worth	₹101 lakh	₹38 lakh		
₹4,800 pm would be worth		₹102 lakh	₹30 lakh	
₹16,300 pm would be worth			₹100 lakh	₹39 lakh
₹42,000 pm would be worth				₹100 lakh

Source: HDFC Mutual Fund Factsheet, January 2019, https://tinyurl.com/3yf7jkar. Accessed on 19 September 2023.

This immense difference in the amount of investment they had to make to build the same corpus was a matter of just 15 years!

From the table above, you can also see that starting to invest just five years later could make a massive difference to the corpus. For example, investing ₹1,800 per month for 25 years will give you a corpus of ₹1.01 crore, but investing the same amount for 20 years will return just ₹38 lakh.

So, what is the moral of the story? Money compounds, and it pays to start investing early. You can invest smaller amounts to get sizable gains. Also, I recommend getting a head start on equity investments. As you grow older, your responsibilities increase. This might dampen your inclination to invest in equities, since a lot more is at stake in life. The end of your income stream, if it is coming from a salary, is much closer. You have more liabilities—home loans, car loans, children's education, household expenses, elderly care for your parents, medical expenses, and so on. Your capacity to take a loss decreases, and so you often end up making investment decisions that do not help you move towards your wealth goals.

I was recently contacted by an elderly couple who had been saving their money in bank FDs their entire lives. Now, when they are in their late 60s, the interest income isn't enough to even meet their monthly expenses! And now they had to figure out how to build a pension from their existing corpus after their retirement. Equities were the only possible asset class that could have given them the desired results, but they had neither the time nor the understanding to make a decision to invest in the asset class. To build wealth, you need to look ahead, plan for the future and have the time that the money needs to multiply.

So, if you haven't thought about wealth creation and financial freedom yet, this is the time to get started! In the next few chapters, we'll talk about how markets work, what you can do to build a corpus of funds, and how to use the 1 per cent formula to live a comfortable life with a 'salary-pension' model.

KEY TAKEAWAYS AND REFLECTIONS

1. The way to wealth is by owning or investing in businesses. You do not need to be a financial genius to do that; you just need to choose wisely and be patient.
2. The upcoming 30 years are touted to be the golden age for Indian investors. We will see a boom in the creation and consumption of goods and services aided by a young population, policy reforms, infrastructure investments and technology.
3. Penetration of goods and services in India is at a fraction of its more developed counterparts—a gap that is starting to fill as access and affordability improves. As consumption grows, so will the profits and, therefore, investor wealth.
4. Leading global agencies have recognized India's potential and put forward highly positive growth estimates.
5. If you do not invest in equities, you lose out on a great opportunity for financial freedom.

CHEW ON THIS

1. What holds you back from investing in equities?
2. How much money are you losing by investing in seemingly safe assets?
3. What happens after you retire?

3

Decoding the Share Market

'An important key to investing is to remember that stocks are not lottery tickets.'

—Peter Lynch

DOES INVESTING IN EQUITIES SCARE YOU?

The richest people in the world are business owners. Shareholders are also part-owners of the same businesses. Yet, the most common experience shared by individuals about share markets is that after some point, they 'burnt their fingers'!

If you look at historical data, share markets have proven to deliver the most attractive returns. Why do these 'burnt fingers' happen then? Why are individual investors not able to achieve the same gains as the main business owners of the same companies? Why are the experiences so varied when it is the same market?

It is all in the mindset!

I've got a quarter century of experience in this industry, and over the years, I have heard the same objections from most individual investors:

'I don't have money to gamble in the stock market.' 'Share

market is only for the rich; I can't afford to lose my money.' 'I don't have the time to monitor the market.' 'It's not a stable investment. If there is a drop, I will lose all my money.'

Most people who invest in share markets do it with the wrong mindset. They want easy money and act on tip-offs to trade shares quickly. That's not a good approach at all! And it, in fact, is akin to gambling!

The owners of businesses, who painstakingly research different aspects of setting up and running their enterprises, also make the effort to constantly update their knowledge about the different factors that may affect their investments. This approach is focussed and long term, and decisions on growing their business are well informed. If you take away one thing from this book, I want you to take away this: share markets are volatile in the short term but not in the long term. Investing in shares is a long-term commitment.

One needs to look at equity investing as 'ownership of businesses'. When you consider investing in the shares of a company, the decision to invest should be based on thorough research about all the aspects of the business, including its future prospects. There may be ups and downs in the share prices in the short term, but as the company grows over the years, so do its profits and your share in them.

But it's difficult not to panic when the markets tank, right? And it happens to the best of us. The nature of the markets is such that it can spring a surprise every now and then. It happened to someone I know as well—let's call her Anaya. She started investing in late 2007 after she got her first job. She put in ₹50,000 in the DSP Flexi-cap Fund and hoped that the money would grow. However, in 2008, the financial crisis happened, the market crashed, and so did the value of her investment. Anaya panicked because this was a significant chunk of her salary and withdrew whatever amount was left. Instead of making a profit, now she was in the red. Having 'burnt her fingers', she swore off investing and did not enter the stock market again till 2016. But like I said, equity investing is a long-term game. If she had not withdrawn her money then, and *stayed invested* in the same MF, her initial ₹50,000 would today (March end, 2023) be ₹2,57,000. The lesson? Stay invested for the long term. And I'm stating this over and over again because this is the core tenet of making money with equities.

Staying put when you see your hard-earned money dwindle takes emotional grit and discipline. Once you acquire the discipline, it becomes a habit.

A lack of this discipline is why most people think investing, especially in equities, is best left to the 'finance guys'. Stock markets intimidate most of us. It looks like such a complex place, with so much data to analyse, risks to evaluate and the possibility that you might make the wrong choice!

That is why more than 90 per cent of household financial savings in India are parked in some kind of assured return investments such as FDs, public provident fund (PPF) and post office or insurance schemes.[1] Around 10 per cent of our savings go into share markets, including MFs as an investment avenue.

The perception of equity markets has mostly been that of volatility, and, hence, people feel it's risky to put their hard-earned money there. Many of those who invest in MFs depend heavily on financial advisors or tips from friends and family.

---

[1]'The Reserve Bank of India Bulletin', *Reserve Bank of India*, March 2021, https://tinyurl.com/4p4jt24a. Accessed on 12 September 2023.

In my two-and-a-half-decade-long journey in the financial sector, I've managed funds for many people, and the ask is always the same: 'you do what you think best.' On the other hand, FDs wear the mantle of stability and reliability. The common thinking is, 'The interest might be low, but at least my principal is safe.' And so, people who invest on their own put their money in these 'safe' instruments. This is a fundamental flaw in how people think about investing!

Let me introduce you to the concept of opportunity cost. Loosely defined, opportunity cost is what you sacrifice when you choose one option over another. For example, let's say you have ₹2,000 that you use to buy a pair of shoes. Your opportunity cost is everything else that you could have done with that money—like go out for dinner, enrol in a course or invest that money.

When you make a less desirable choice, the opportunity cost adds up. For example, if you have an hour, you could spend it:

A) Working, which will earn you ₹5,000
B) Partying, which will cost you ₹2,000

In this case, if you choose Option B, the opportunity cost (in monetary terms) is ₹7,000. Therefore,

> Opportunity cost = The money you spend + Loss of the money you could have earned

This is just an example. I'm definitely not recommending that you choose work over recreation all the time. In fact, this book aspires to help you do the opposite! But I hope you understand the idea of opportunity cost.

OPPORTUNITY COST OF FIXED/ASSURED RETURN INVESTMENTS

When you choose to invest in seemingly safe investment instruments like FDs, you lose out on the higher returns that MFs can give you. Assuming an FD gives an 8 per cent interest per annum, and EMFs about 15–18 per cent CAGR, you lose out on 7–10 per cent interest per annum! That is a lot of money to forgo in one year. Imagine how much it adds up to in your lifetime!

Power of compounding with a difference of just 2%		
₹1,00,000/- compounding @	Wealth in 15 Years (in lakh)	Wealth in 25 Years (in lakh)
7%	2.76	5.43
9%	3.64	8.62
11%	4.78	13.59
13%	6.25	21.23
15%	8.14	32.92

And this is not just a hypothesis; historical data is proof. Let's say, in 1998, you invested ₹10,000 in bank FDs and ₹10,000 in the Franklin India (FI) Flexi-cap Fund. What would your balance be in 2023? See Table 3 for the answer!

Table 3
Difference in wealth in 25 years—Bank FD vs EMF

31 March	Bank FD	FI Flexi-cap Fund
1998	10,000	10,000
2003	15,348	28,195
2008	20,631	1,99,218
2013	30,404	2,97,883
2018	44,769	7,06,059
2023	59,342	12,10,794

Source: Data for bank FDs is from RBI; data for FI Flexi-cap Cap Fund is from Franklin Templeton NAV data.

Well, the bank FD would be just over ₹59,000, while the fund's value would be over ₹12,00,000! That's more than 20 times the returns over the FD in the 25 years.

But people take the 'safe' bet time and again because they are not thinking about money the right way. They fear loss and do not realize that they are bound to lose a lot of money by not making the right investment choices.

Over time, that loss adds up.

Investing in bank FDs is not a mistake in itself. A certain portion of your savings should be free of any risk—and the percentage can vary depending on individual risk profiles. The thumb rule is that risk-free investments bring in the least possible returns. Putting the majority or all of your savings in an asset class that, post-tax and post inflation, gives a negative return is certainly a mistake!

And this is what made me write this book—to share with you a simple formula for financial freedom that does not require you to be a financial whiz kid; to help you build healthy investing habits; to help you invest your money wisely and make the most of the golden goose that is India's economic opportunity.

INVESTING FROM A DIFFERENT LENS

We've looked at some of the reasons why people shy away from investing in equities, the fears they operate from and the cost they end up paying by not leveraging the amazing opportunity that is India's growth story. However, business owners and shareholders have different experiences of returns while being invested in the same business. The lens with which one views equity investing can make all the difference in returns.

We've touched upon the two ways to invest in India's growth story—be a full-time business owner or become a shareholder

Investing from a Different Lens

and part-time owner of an established business. Ownership comes with responsibility. But, interestingly, business owners and shareholders tend to look at this differently.

A Typical Share Trader's Lens

Vinay is a senior executive in a multinational fast-moving consumer goods (FMCG) company. He is the brand manager of a very profitable product that the company owns. He invested most of his earnings in shares. What had started as a hobby became a serious investment avenue for him. He was in touch with three different broking firms that were a constant source of 'fresh ideas' for him to invest in.

At any given time, Vinay's 'portfolio' has anywhere between 20 to 30 companies' shares. While he has had a few bad experiences in the past, he is quite thrilled with his overall experience. In his social circles, he couldn't stop talking about DEFG Co. Ltd., a software company. He bought its shares at ₹2 per share and, within a two-month period, it shot up to ₹43. What a 'multi-bagger'!

This had been the year 1999 and the Y2K phenomenon had jacked up the share prices of any company in the IT sector—or even remotely related to the field. It was a frenzy! Everybody was buying IT shares, and prices were doubling every month.

One day, Vinay's relationship manager at FRFR Brokers Pvt. Ltd called him to share this great 'tip' about HIJK Soft*wear* Ltd—a company with an upcoming IPO at ₹10 per share.

Vinay could not believe what he heard! An IT company's share at just ₹10 in such frenzied times was just a bonanza. It was a goldmine! There were rumours in the market that post the IPO, the share would open at 30 or more, and since not many knew about this company, full allotment to his subscription was guaranteed.

HIJK Softwear

Based on the tip, Vinay sold most of his other portfolio and invested it in this company. His objective? Make a quick buck.

What Vinay did is not called investing. It's gambling. He didn't spend any time or effort in understanding what he was investing in. He didn't consider the long-term gains of any of his existing investments. He just wanted to switch his bets on what he was told was a winning horse.

This is the approach that leads to losses. Business owners take a very different route to investments.

THE BUSINESS OWNER'S LENS

Amit is a second-generation entrepreneur. In the late 1980s, his father had started a small-scale unit for manufacturing plastic bags that later expanded to corrugated boxes and plastic bottles. Amit joined the family business after doing his MBA in 2000. He spent the first few years understanding the intricacies of the business and dived deeper into every aspect of the packaging industry—production challenges, new technologies, eco-trends in demand, supply and distribution, demand trends for new industries, finance, etc. He became a regular at the annual International Pack Expo in Chicago, USA, to keep himself up to date on the latest happenings in the industry across the world.

Amit's ambition was to take the company to great heights. In 2008, he commissioned a fully automated machine, which he had imported from France. This machine increased the production capacity of the plant from ₹50 crore to ₹300 crore per annum. Seeing great potential in the business, he decided to make the company public. Today, Rewari and Sons Ltd. is a listed company with large-scale production capabilities, catering to all kinds of packaging needs of the FMCG and Pharma industries across India. The company boasts of having the most sophisticated manufacturing plants with the latest world-class technology.

Amit's family owns 65 per cent of the shares in this business that is on a fast-track to growth, and he relentlessly works and invests in growing the company. His objective? Wealth creation for self and future generations.

There was a new investment opportunity for Rewari and Sons Ltd. Amit researched and found packaged drinking water to be a good area of expansion. He studied trends in this sector and was aware of the rising demand. He knew that the increasing awareness of chemical and bacteria pollution and right pH levels in drinking water, combined with rising affordability within the large Indian middle-class population, meant a great opportunity for the segment. Survey reports indicated that this market would grow at 30 per cent per annum for the next five years. Amit knew that even with a few well-established players in the market, there is room for many more.

He undertook an extensive exercise to research and understand what he was getting into. His feasibility study covered aspects of every area of the business. What would he need for manufacturing, sales and marketing, and distribution and logistics? What were the legal and compliance factors? What were the financial implications? What would be the return on this investment?

Do you see the difference?

Amit didn't go and invest in the expansion based on a market tip. He took the time and effort to understand what this investment means and how it will generate wealth for him. He knows that the returns will not be immediate. Setting up and running a business takes time. And Amit is in it for the long run.

As per an old adage, *time in the market beats timing the market.*

Don't Be Vinay

Most of the time, individuals buy shares on 'tips'; that is where the 'experience' starts to go wrong. When you buy shares from the stock exchange, you forget that you have become a part of the business. You do not realize that you are now part-owner of the company.

Dr Anuranjan Bist, my school friend and a psychiatrist, told me:

> A greed- and fear-based approach to equity investing is akin to gambling and triggers two responses. Some people, feeling that the markets are 'rigged' choose to opt out and not invest in equities at all. And others get addicted to the gamble—the compulsive need to keep pouring in money in the markets, without any rhyme or reason, to get that high of winning.

As a responsible investor of your hard-earned money, you need to understand the dynamics of the business before investing. Don't base your investment decisions on emotions and general sentiment, rather analyse and make sense of where you are about to put your money.

WHAT MAKES EQUITY INVESTING DIFFICULT FOR THE INDIVIDUAL INVESTOR?

The study of individual businesses and the intricacies of share markets require extensive research. But analysing every stock is difficult given the massive size of the Indian share market. There are over 5,000 listed companies categorized in around 30 broad sectors. There are more than 11,000 FIIs, 42 MF companies, 57 insurance companies and crores of individual investors that participate in our share markets valued at a total of around $3 trillion.

It requires the effort of an entire institution to research and constantly track what's happening in the market—something individual investors cannot do alone.

And so, when it comes to equity, they need to take expert advice. The best way for an individual investor to participate in the equity markets is through MFs.

Another thing that makes share market investing complicated is the nature of returns. In the case of a bank FD, the bank confirms and guarantees the returns on your investment beforehand. The investor knows how much return they will get before they put their money in. In the case of shares, returns are based on the future profit of the company.

Return = Profit per share or Earnings per share (EPS)

40 • *Gain Your Financial Freedom with the 1% Formula*

Navigating the Complexity of Equity Markets

And, the investor cannot know these exact profits before they invest. Their investment decision is based on an estimate of what these profits could be. And not everyone is tuned in to the business landscape enough to excel at this estimation game.

Finally, an individual investor finds it challenging to stick to the fundamentals of stock investing—'buy low, sell high'. It's common sense to buy shares at a lower price and sell them when the price appreciates. Instead, they try and time the markets with the wrong dominant emotion clouding their decision making.

Let's say you have been watching a share rise due to some favourable news related to the company. Say that the price rose from ₹100 to ₹120. Now, the same favourable reason creates a perception that prices will go up even further, and this dominant emotion of greed will urge you to buy at the higher price (₹120).

Now consider the reverse. Let's say, a few months after you bought the share, the price fell due to some unfavourable news about the company. Say that it slid to ₹80. Due to the same reason that the price fell in the first place, the fear of the price falling further becomes the dominant emotion, urging you to sell at the lower price (₹80).

Due to the wrong emotion at work at the wrong time, you did the exact opposite of the recommended advice, that is, buy low, sell high! You bought high and sold low. Most people do that.

The human mind is prone to disregard common sense when it comes to stock-market investing. There is an urge to try and time the market. When the markets are high, people have an irresistible temptation to buy shares in line with the euphoric general sentiment. And when the market goes to red, there is a self-destructive, panic-induced urge to sell. I've seen it happen to many people. This is especially prevalent when a crisis strikes and markets tank in scenarios like the 2008 global financial crisis or the 2020 Covid-19 induced fall in share prices. I have seen that the urge of trying to time the markets always works against the best interests of the investor.

I had just on-boarded a couple, Mr and Mrs Lodha, as a client in early 2020, just before the Covid-19 crisis hit. A couple of months after they invested their money, the markets fell to a record low in years. The Sensex was at a multi-year low of 25,981 on 23 March 2020, down from the 41,000-mark it touched in January 2020—a shocking dip of about 30 per cent—perhaps, the worst ever recorded. The Lodhas, predictably, were in panic. They had lost 30 per cent of the value of their original investment. And they wanted to cut their losses and get out of the market to probably come back when markets 'stabilized' at 'lower levels'. This was clearly not a good move. But reining in rash decisions when the clients see their money erode is difficult. They persisted in their decision and withdrew. If they had stayed invested for just a few months, they would have left with gains instead of losses. They never found the 'lower levels' to come back again—the Sensex made an impressive recovery, rebounding to the earlier high of 41,000 and then went on to make fresh all-time-high levels throughout to eventually close the year at the level of 48,000.

It is cases like these that have prompted me to write this book. I want to decode stock investing for individual investors and help you make rational decisions to benefit from this asset class. I want you to understand how stock markets really work. I want you to know the basic principles on which stock markets operate so that you can base your investment decisions on rationale, and not let emotions cloud your judgment.

And that's what this chapter is about.

THE FOUR PRINCIPLES OF SHARE MARKETS

During the second half of my 15-year stint there, my company had become the largest MF house in the country. We were very proud of having built the country's strongest fund management teams with 11 sector analysts, nine dealers, nine fund managers and a chief investment officer who went on to become one of the world's longest-serving fund managers for a single MF scheme.

Collectively, this team had over 400 years of experience in market research and fund management across multiple cycles of the markets. We monitored the business trends in each sector and studied any changes in the policy environment and its implications for that sector.

Individual companies were tracked through periodic meetings with their management, competitors, dealers and other stakeholders to analyse their strengths and weaknesses. Their financials were analysed constantly, and so were their stock prices. Most importantly, the governance standards and professionalism credentials were established first, and only then a company was approved to the 'core list' of investment-worthy enterprises. The team of dealers kept tabs on inflow and outflow trends of institutions and retail investors—foreign and local. The debt markets team had even developed an in-house ratings system, a practice that would match that of any of the largest ratings agencies in the world.

It was one of the most robust risk management systems that one could think of, and, over time, the team has built interesting ways to keep themselves on top of things. For example, one of our analysts who tracked the auto sector had the most enviable task to personally test-drive all newly launched vehicles to gauge the future successes of the companies. Our cement-sector analysts would travel to the four corners of the country, not only to meet the executives of big cement companies, but also to meet their dealers, related real-estate companies and infrastructure companies. This provided them a first-hand all-round understanding of the demand trends in the sector. Our IT and pharma groups would travel overseas to gauge the demand trends in the economies that these sectors export to. The team had a wealth of knowledge about all the building blocks that go into the making of the Indian economy!

To synergize the business of the company, I interacted with the fund management team and always enjoyed the conversations with them. I was curious to connect the dots between market performance and investor experience—to find the missing link between the growth of our carefully selected, most valuable companies and the layman understanding of how stock markets work.

I discussed my experiences of investor behaviour during various market cycles—during the frenzied times and the big crashes, the Asian financial crisis, the dot-com boom, the US sub-prime crisis, 9/11, elections, wars and other such events. We exchanged thoughts on how markets as a whole react during such times; how different segments of the market behave; how experts, who have witnessed such events in the past, act; and how individual investors behave.

I have come to believe that while every event, every cycle will be different from the last one, there are certain principles on which the markets will work. I have synthesized all my learnings from all my interactions with some of the best minds in the industry into the four principles of share markets. These are guiding principles to anyone who would like to unravel the mystery behind why markets are behaving in the manner that they are during a given situation.

To understand how share markets work, you need to understand the four principles that govern share markets.

Principle 1: Markets Are Forward Looking

We discussed how share price valuations work on the principle of estimating future profits. An investor invests in a share depending on whether the series of estimated future profits justify the share price today. Share market professionals constantly analyse companies' performance trajectory and estimate the profits of companies for as long as they can. This exercise is not restricted to just a year; profits are estimated over two or three years—and sometimes more—in order to support the decision to buy, sell or hold. This constant endeavour to keep analysing the future is second nature to every market participant.

The estimation process begins with the projections made by the concerned company's management in its business plans. Individual analysts can then formulate their own opinion about the projections and arrive at estimated profit figures—be it higher or lower. They constantly track all the variable factors that may affect the future profitability of a company. Any change is quantified into a change in the future profit figure, resulting in a new 'adjusted share price' figure.

While short-term events that alter the business situation of companies do require careful analysis for their effect on the profitability of companies, market participants are quick to quantify such events and build it into the share price to eventually move on to their second nature—looking forward!

Markets look to the future from a major event much before the effect of that event is neutralized. For instance, during the Covid-19 crisis in 2020, the resulting uncertainty caused the markets to dip, but they began to lift as soon as talks around a vaccine made the news. By the time of the second Covid-19 wave in 2021, analysts had already seen the positive effect of vaccinations play out in other countries and the time taken to develop herd immunity, rather than focus on the spike in cases and the lockdowns!

Principle 2: Markets Do Not Like Uncertainty

Over years of experience, professional research analysts develop the ability to quantify the impact of variable factors that affect a business—something that individual investors should take guidance from. Such events could be a change in policy or environment, failure of a newly launched product of the company, new competition, labour unrest or the approval of a new license. It could be just about anything that can eventually be measured, impacting the profits—positively or negatively!

Some events have a direct and measurable impact on profitability, for example, change in taxation percentage. Other events may have an indirect, yet, to some extent measurable, impact, for instance, certain protectionist measures announced in a foreign country where the clients of the company are located.

However, there are some events that can create a very high level of uncertainty, where the impact on profits may not be quantifiable immediately, for example, the outbreak of a pandemic. This restricts the ability of the markets to look forward, which is not an ideal situation as per Principle 1, and can create sharp negative reactions in the markets: the higher the level of uncertainty, the sharper the reaction.

As an individual investor, you need to understand that markets may fall each time there is uncertainty. However, instead of getting dissuaded by the uncertainty and not investing or withdrawing from the market, you should see that as an opportunity to put in more money. For example, uncertainty due to the US elections in 2020 led to a market drop. However, whichever way the outcome would have gone, corporate profitability in India would not have been impacted, especially in the non-export sectors (85 per cent of the GDP that time), which means the share prices would have rebounded to normal/higher levels eventually. And they did!

However, in volatile markets, it is important that you create a cushion for your financial goals. We will talk about this in later chapters.

Principle 3: In the Long Term, Share Prices Track Profit Growth

To understand this principle, let's first understand how share prices work. Like any other investment, there is simple mathematics at the core, that is, for a principal amount invested, there is a return percentage.

Hypothetically, for a bank FD that gives 7 per cent interest per annum,

Principal amount = ₹100
Return = ₹7
Return percentage = 7/100 = 7% (as promised)

Equivalence can be established in terms of shares as well. Consider the following scenario:

Principal amount = Share price = ₹100 per share
Return = Profits = Profits per share, that is, earnings per share (EPS) = ₹12
Return percentage = Return/Principal = EPS/Share Price
= 12/100 = 12%

Let's freeze the 12 per cent returns expectation as constant to understand the correlation between share prices and profit growth.

Year	Share Price	Profits/EEPS	Return
2009	100	12	12%

Now, in 10 years, if profits rise five times from EPS ₹12 to EPS ₹60, this is how share prices will rise to give the 12 per cent return.

Year	Share Price	Profits/EPS	Returns
2009	100	12	12%
2019	500	60	12%

So, a five-fold rise in profits has resulted in a five-fold increase in share price!

Let's look at the other situation where, due to some reason, profits were to fall over a 10-year period, let's say 25 per cent, from EPS ₹12 to EPS ₹9; this is how share prices will change to give a 12 per cent return.

Year	Share Price	Profits/EPS	Returns
2009	100	12	12%
2019	75	9	12%

This time, a 25 per cent fall in profits has resulted in a 25 per cent fall in share price!

In the long term, markets seem to follow this principle of tracking only the profit growth. It acts more like a guiding principle in the short term, however, when there are a variety of factors driving markets.

Of course, the returns expectations are not fixed—that was just an example to illustrate a point. Different people have different expectations of returns, and that is why a trade happens. Even for a single person, return expectations can change based on changes in the economic landscape. Since equities are considered to be a risky asset class, the expectation is to receive some extra returns over the risk-free bank FD returns. So, for instance, if the bank FD rates are at 5 per cent, then an equity return of 10 per cent is good, too. However, if bank FD rates become 10 per cent, then the return expectation from equity could rise to 15–18 per cent. A change in the risk-free returns changes the expectations from the equity market, a riskier asset class

Now consider this—when interest rates rise and expectations from equities also rises, there is no way any company can start generating more profits just because the expectations have risen, so share prices fall. In the following equation, to increase returns, since we cannot increase the numerator (profits), we decrease the denominator (share price):

Returns = Profits/Share price

So, when general interest rates rise, equity prices fall because of the higher expectation from the asset class.

Principle 4: In the Short Term, Markets Are Volatile

While markets tend to follow some mathematical constructs in the long term, they are anything but a perfect science in the short term.

If profits drive share prices, in a perfect world, the share price of a company should change only once every quarter when the results are announced. In reality, share prices fluctuate every second on a given trading day.

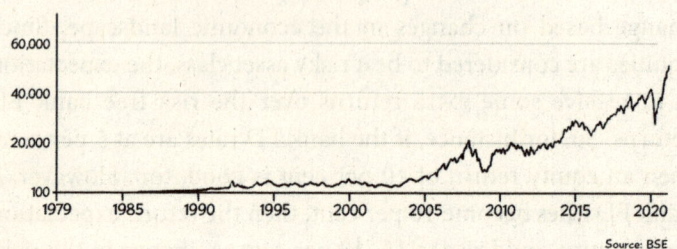

Sensex over the long term–four decades

Source: BSE

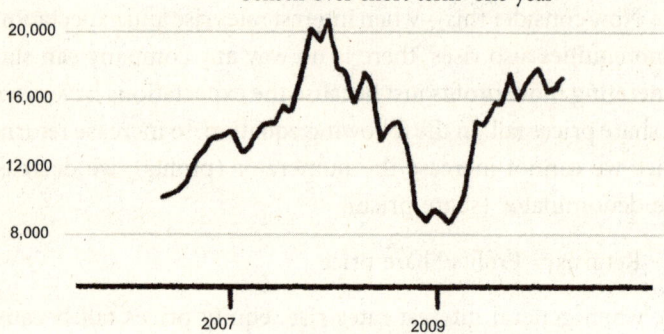

Sensex over short term–one year

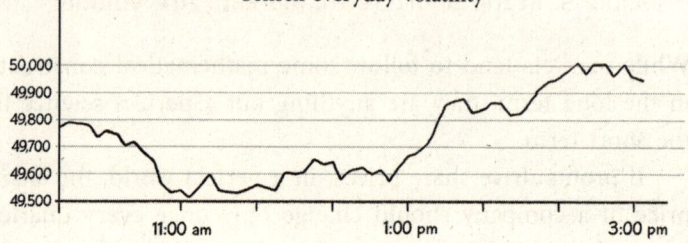

Sensex everyday volatility

Markets, in general, are prone to demand–supply factors. So, the price fluctuates when large institutional players or promoters buy or sell large quantities of stock of a particular company. Change in risk-free rates can change the expectation of returns from equity, impacting the share price. Rumours of takeovers, bankruptcy and 'insider information' can also cause fluctuations in share prices. International events affect market sentiment, too. For instance, the news of 9/11 in the US caused a huge crash in global markets, which was corrected later.

Obviously, unforeseen events cause fluctuations in share prices, but such events also do not happen as frequently as the change in prices. Short-term volatility is in the very nature of stock trading.

At any given point of time in the equity markets, there are broadly two sets of factors at play. Both may seem to have strong logic for prices to move in a certain direction:

1. Business fundamentals: These include all those factors that affect the earnings and the profit growth of a company. They can be quantifiable to the extent that they affect the profitability of the company.
2. Sentiment factors: These are mostly non-quantifiable factors that, by the very definition of the category, affect the sentiment towards the performance of the company, sector or share markets as a whole.

The short-term volatility is also dependent on how traders perceive the market. Trade happens when there are two people with opposite views on the share price movement at the same price point. The buyer has the view that the share price will rise from where it is at, and the seller anticipates a fall. These views are based on the business or sentimental factors and can be logical or illogical.

Logical

BUYER	SELLER
Has a higher estimate of profits	Has a lower estimate of profits
Has a lower expectation of returns (8%)	Has a higher expectation of returns (12%)

Illogical

BUYER	SELLER
An employee of the company. Has emotional attachment to owning the stock	Reads a social media article interpreted as negative for the company

Often, market sentiment is also driven by ignorance. This happened with a company called Bombay Oxygen.[2] When news of the Covid-19–related oxygen shortage was in the limelight, the share prices of Bombay Oxygen shot up by two-and-a-half times in a couple of weeks. The funny thing is that this company has nothing to do with oxygen! In reality, it was a non-banking financial corporation (NBFC) since 2019 and had nothing to contribute to oxygen supplies.

The most certain and predictable thing about equities is that they are volatile in the short term. Later in the book, we will discuss why these short-term factors are quite irrelevant for us in our quest for building wealth!

---

[2] 'Investing in Covid: Bombay Oxygen soars to Rs 24,574 per share. It has nothing to do with Oxygen', *ET Now News*, 20 April 2021, https://tinyurl.com/258mzzwe. Accessed on 13 September 2023.

How Our Markets Have Displayed These Principles

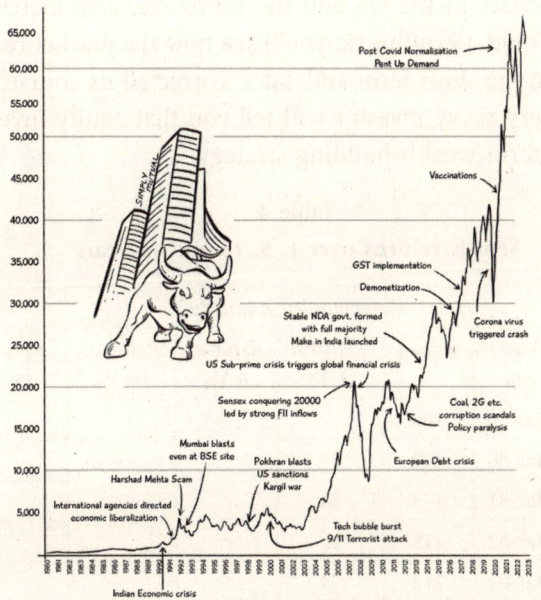

The Journey of Sensex

If we take real data of the market index, we can see these principles in action.

Table 4 lists the Sensex returns over the course of one year, five years, 10 years and 15 years. If you notice the returns for one year alone, there is a lot of volatility (Principle 4) and, in some years, negative returns. In fact, in 44 financial years, there were positive returns in only 30. This makes share market investing tricky and a risky gamble for the short-term investor. However, if you see the returns over five, 10 and 15 years, the probability of gains keeps increasing, finally becoming 100 per cent if you stay invested for 15 years—no matter how the markets behaved in the interim. If you also see the journey of Sensex over the years with key events such as elections, financial crises in the US and the Eurozone, demonetization and the Covid-19 outbreak, you'll see how the market reacted to them in the short term and, later, corrected its course. This is why every savvy investor will tell you that equity investing is a long-term wealth-building strategy.

Table 4
Sensex returns over 1, 5, 10 and 15 years

			Compounded Annually			
No. of years	*Year end*	Sensex	*Returns: 1 Yr*	*Returns: 5 Yrs*	*Returns: 10 Yrs*	*Returns: 15 Yrs*
0	Mar-79	100				
1	Mar-80	129	29			
2	Mar-81	173	34			
3	Mar-82	218	26			
4	Mar-83	212	-3			
5	Mar-84	245	16	20		
6	Mar-85	354	44	22		
7	Mar-86	574	62	27		
8	Mar-87	510	-11	19		
9	Mar-88	398	-22	13		
10	Mar-89	714	79	24	22	
11	Mar-90	781	9	17	20	
12	Mar-91	1,168	50	15	21	
13	Mar-92	4,285	267	53	35	
14	Mar-93	2,281	-47	42	27	
15	Mar-94	3,779	66	40	31	27
16	Mar-95	3,261	-14	33	25	24
17	Mar-96	3,367	3	24	19	22

Compounded Annually						
No. of years	Year end	Sensex	Returns: 1 Yr	Returns: 5 Yrs	Returns: 10 Yrs	Returns: 15 Yrs
18	Mar-97	3,361	0	-5	21	20
19	Mar-98	3,893	16	11	26	21
20	Mar-99	3,740	-4	0	18	20
21	Mar-00	5,001	34	9	20	19
22	Mar-01	3,604	-28	1	12	13
23	Mar-02	3,469	-4	1	-2	14
24	Mar-03	3,049	-12	-5	3	15
25	Mar-04	5,591	83	8	4	15
26	Mar-05	6,493	16	5	7	15
27	Mar-06	11,280	74	26	13	16
28	Mar-07	13,072	16	30	15	8
29	Mar-08	15,644	20	39	15	14
30	Mar-09	9,709	-38	12	10	6
31	Mar-10	17,528	81	22	13	12
32	Mar-11	19,445	11	12	18	12
33	Mar-12	17,404	-10	6	18	12
34	Mar-13	18,836	8	4	20	11
35	Mar-14	22,386	19	18	15	13
36	Mar-15	27,957	25	10	16	12
37	Mar-16	25,342	-9	5	8	14
38	Mar-17	29,621	17	11	9	15
39	Mar-18	32,969	11	12	8	17
40	Mar-19	38,673	17	12	15	14
41	Mar-20	29,468	-24	1	5	11
42	Mar-21	49,509	68	14	10	10
43	Mar-22	58,569	18	15	13	11

Compounded Annually						
No. of years	Year end	Sensex	Returns: 1 Yr	Returns: 5 Yrs	Returns: 10 Yrs	Returns: 15 Yrs
44	Mar-23	58,992	1	12	12	9
Probability of Gains			30 in 44	36 in 39	34 in 35	30 in 30

Source: Data collated by the author

With the year-end data from March 2020 and Mar 2021 in Table 4, it's also clear that markets are forward looking (Principle 1). While the pandemic was still prevailing, the news of development of a vaccine shot up returns from negative 24 per cent to positive 68 per cent!

Also, if you see Table 4, you'll notice that uncertainty causes markets to go down (Principle 2). See the 24 per cent dip in returns in 2020 due to the Covid-19 crisis, one of the most uncertain times, not just for markets but for mankind as well. The dip from the pre-pandemic high of 41,000 in February 2020 to a low of 25,981 on 23 March was actually a fall of 37 per cent in just a month due to extreme uncertainty.

But over the course of the years, markets track profit growth (Principle 3). Let us take the massive 267 per cent returns in the Harshad Mehta scam period of 1992, for instance, and the slump that followed. This was a time when markets grew 10 times in a period of four years—much more than the profit growth rate. Since the markets had run up much more than profits, it took many years after that with no movement in prices till profits caught up. The GDP is an indicator of corporate profitability. In the last four decades, the nominal GDP growth, that is, GDP using current prices without adjusting for inflation, has been in the range of 12–15 per cent (see Figure 4). And if you see the table for market returns over the 15-year period, they also converge to a similar range. To look at yet another instance—the 15-year returns as of end-March 2023—the 9 per cent figure seems to be reflecting one of the lowest growth rates. If we look back, this period covers two very impactful, GDP-growth-slowing events—the global financial crisis and the Covid pandemic—both causing slowdown in the economy, which was reflected in the Sensex returns.

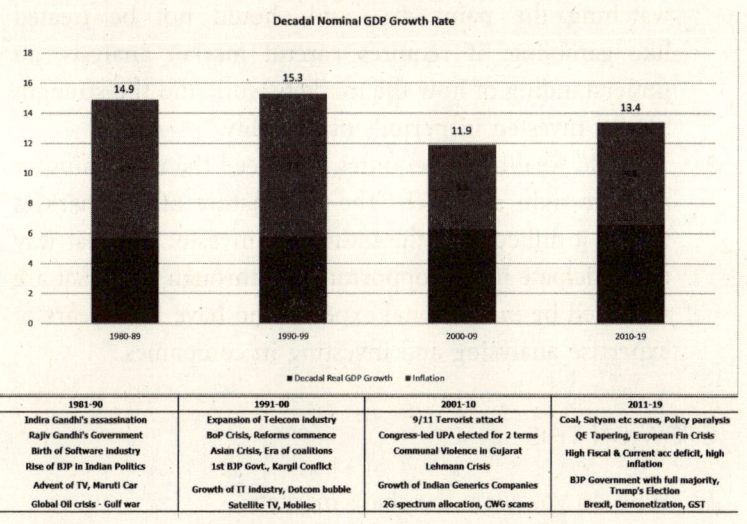

Figure 4: Decadal nominal GDP growth rate

Source: Data calculated by the author from 'Inflation, Consumer Prices (Annual %)—India', *The World Bank*, https://tinyurl.com/4cwyz4wh. Accessed on 27 September 2023; 'GDP Growth (Annual %)—India', *The World Bank*, https://tinyurl.com/2p9crkew. Accessed on 27 September 2023.

KEY TAKEAWAYS AND REFLECTIONS

1. Markets work on four key principles:
   a) Markets are forward looking
   b) Markets do not like uncertainty
   c) In the long term, share prices track profit growth
   d) In the short term, markets are volatile
2. Equity investing is a long-term game of patience—like watching the paint dry—and should not be treated like gambling. It requires careful market analysis, an understanding of how the markets work and the strength to stay invested in periods of volatility.
3. To build wealth with equities, you need the right mindset and the right approach. The very nature of the markets makes it difficult for the individual investor. A great way to participate in this opportunity is through MFs that are managed by institutional experts who have built years of expertise analysing and investing in companies.

CHEW ON THIS

1. How do you view the share markets?
2. How do you invest in the share markets?
3. What can you do better in terms of equity investing?

4

The Money Mindset

In the previous chapter, we saw how stock markets work on four key principles. Two of the main principles outlined were long-term growth and short-term volatility. That sounds simple enough, right? So why do so many individual investors either shy away from share markets or 'burn their fingers'? To understand that, we need to dive deeper into the psychology of money. In order to do so, I approached my friend Dr Anuranjan Bist, a psychiatrist certified by the American Board of Medical Specialties.

Anuranjan and I go way back. Beginning with our *La Martiniere* days, our friendship has survived the test of time and distance. Anuranjan went on to become the founder and CEO of the Mind Brain Institute, Las Vegas, USA, after attaining his master's in Public Health with an emphasis on psychiatric public health at the University of South Carolina and finishing his residency at the Brookdale University Hospital, New York, USA.

He has a deep personal interest in 'investor psychology', and we have had many interesting conversations, ranging from investor behaviour to addiction in rats! In fact, I have been bouncing off the idea of this book with him for a while now, and that's how we got talking about the money mindset. Here's what he had to say:

> It's the very nature of share markets and the principles that they operate on that makes it difficult for the individual investor to participate in them. Long-term thinking is just not coded into our DNA! Human brains are wired to think about the here-and-now, about short-term survival. We have spent hundreds of thousands of years learning to survive day by day as hunter-gatherers. There was no long-term planning then. And that's the way our brains have evolved—to focus on the day-to-day.
>
> In comparison, the stock markets are just a blip on our time scale, having been in existence for just a few hundred years. So even when we understand logic, instinct makes it difficult for us to follow it.
>
> Instead of thinking of long-term gains, we start operating from two key emotions—fear and greed. And acting on these emotions is driven by social pressure and group thinking. What other people say and do have a significant effect on us. When everyone talks about something, we start believing in it. And it's very difficult to go against it. And that again ties back to our origins. As hunter-gatherers, humans could not survive outside of the tribe. Even today, if everyone we know is doing something, we end up doing it too.
>
> So, when the stock market is at its peak, everyone talks about it. We hear it in conversations, we see it in the media, we may know some people who made money in the stock market—and that's when greed shows up. If everyone is benefitting, it must be good, right? And so, we dive in and invest in stocks.

Herd Mentality

Later, when the markets course correct from a peak, fear comes in. Fear is a powerful emotion, and it hijacks the logical part of the brain. So even when common sense says, 'Stay invested when the market is low', fear says, 'Take your money out!' Most people give in to that fear and, as a result, lose money.

What's more, the market is self-perpetuating. So, if it's falling and people take out money, it slides further and creates more fear. In the short term, then, these human emotions end up dictating the market.

One thing about fear is that, unlike happiness, it is essential for survival. Fear is what kept humans alive in those early days. The negative information told us what was dangerous and what could kill us. And that instinct has been branded onto our genes. This explains much of our behaviour related to money. For us, the fear of losing a rupee is greater than our pleasure in gaining two rupees. Fear overrides happiness when it comes to decision-making. This is why we have the urge to invest in assured income products where the returns are fixed. It's a guarantee, and that's important to our brains.

In terms of how our brains work, the intangibility of stock market gains also plays a role in choosing not to invest in it. Assets like gold and real estate are tangible and feel 'safer' than just a number changing every second. It takes a long time for any kind of market appreciation to happen, and that's not evident in the day-to-day movement. So, for stocks, we get a sense of the volatility, and it does not feel that safe. And that, again, is because our brain is not coded for the long-term. It compares what happened yesterday to what's happening now and wants to make safe decisions in the now. It cannot visualize the possibilities of what's going to happen a few years from now. And hence, long-term investing requires more discipline.

It's interesting, isn't it? It's not really our inclination towards finance or our knowledge of the sector that stands in our way, but our very biology! We are still held back by the instincts of our hunter-gatherer ancestors! But there must be a way around it, right? If we are not wired to think of long-term gains, how can we consciously invoke this thought process? And that was my next question to Dr Bist.

I would say the first thing in terms of getting the long-term thinking mindset is to introspect on what we want in life. Most of us just live life as a series of daily activities without really thinking of what we want to do in life—what our purpose is. And it might sound strange in a book about finances but knowing what we want in life is extremely important to build the mindset of going out and getting it. Most of us today struggle with unhappiness. We go about doing our jobs despite having a sense of dissatisfaction. That's because we have not stopped to ask ourselves, 'What do I want?', 'What will I be doing in 10, 15, or 20 years from now?' or 'What would make me happy?'

Having clarity in your mind about your life goals will mean that you will eventually establish a set of financial goals as well. Then all you need to achieve those goals is to devise a disciplined approach to investing, where emotions can be kept out of the process.

When we set up auto-debit mandates for SIPs, money is automatically debited from our bank account and invested in an MF scheme of our choice. If you set the auto-debit mandate to coincide with your salary-credit date, then the money goes out before you can pay attention to it; it doesn't feel like a loss because you didn't register the presence of that money in the first place. This brings about a good investment discipline and adapts your spending to the money you actually have in hand.

In stock-market investing, it is a good practice to not track the market daily. Think of it like any other tangible asset and look only at the value of your equity investments over longer time frames—perhaps, an annual review. And if you are able to cut out the noise, build the discipline of investing, and stop worrying about the daily performance, before you know it, ten years would have flown by and you would have a sizable corpus waiting for you.

Equity investing is like any other healthy habit that you need to build. Sure, it will be uncomfortable initially, like when you just start running to stay fit. But if you keep it up, very soon you'll be doing much better and running longer distances. The key is to be disciplined and patient, and to keep at it like a subconscious habit.

Finally, it is clear that you need to know what you want in life and where you want to be before you can start thinking of long-term wealth building. But that's a foresight most people lack. During my stint at HDFC Mutual Fund, my team undertook this exercise during investor conferences where we would ask investors questions about their plans.

We'd ask, 'What would you be doing tomorrow?', and people would have a reasonably certain answer.

We'd ask, 'What would you be doing this week? This month? This year?', and people would still know what they wanted to do.

But as we started asking, 'What would you be doing five to ten years from now?', the answers became less and less concrete.

Then, we pointed out that equities are the exact opposite of this thought process. You need to know what you would be invested in 20 years from now, and not what you would trade in tomorrow.

So, in life, short term is predictable but long term is not; while in equities, long term is predictable but short term is not.

The inability to align to this thought process is why most people are unable to use equity investing to generate wealth.

The next chapter will introduce you to the 1 per cent formula that will help you overcome these money mindset challenges and invest in line with the market principles and your goals.

But first, we need to define your life goals and financial goals.

WHAT ARE YOUR GOALS?

As children, our dreams are fantasies—of fairy-tale lands, mythical creatures and magical happenings. Our young minds have not been exposed to material constraints or the impossibilities of practicality. When we grow up, we still have dreams—the difference is that our dreams come closer to the realm of reality. Our dreams, now, are an extension of what we are, to what we would like to become—an extension of what we have experienced in the world and what we would like to do to change it to make it a world of our dreams. The child in us may still not consider all material requirements to fulfil those dreams, but it is not all magic and illusion. We believe that we have it in us to make it happen one day.

One of the most inspiring theories on human psychology is that of self-actualization, something I talked about right at the start. Psychologist Abraham Maslow asserts that humans are inherently motivated to fulfil their potential in life. He also established the idea of a hierarchy of needs. Before one can pursue the highest need of self-actualization, the lower hierarchy needs have to be met—the needs of food, shelter, security, relationships with friends and family, social acceptance and social acceptance and recognition.

Food, Shelter... and a Ferrari

As opposed to the popular saying, good things in life are not only 'not free' but also quite expensive. This means that most of us spend our entire lives lost in the rat race of making a livelihood. The pursuit of money starts with need for basic necessities, then some luxuries and then some. There are also societal norms to follow and family needs to fulfil. The idea of saving for the future creeps in, and no amount of money seems enough. After all, there are the uncertainties of rising costs, children's education, healthcare of loved ones and self, housing needs, emergencies, and all the needs after retirement. We even start wishing never to retire just so that the income may continue lifelong.

We talked about how money is just a means to an end. But in reality, in our pursuit to accumulate the means, we tend to lose sight of the goals, our dreams. There is no time to plan that vacation break, no time to visit family, little time to take care of our health and, most importantly, no time for ourselves to pursue our passions.

Some of us dream of travelling the whole world one day; some dream of becoming a chef and starting a restaurant, maybe pursue wildlife photography; others aspire to work for the environment, or perhaps just doing our own thing, being our own boss! But faced with the worries of making a living, these dreams start fading away.

Is there a way to live better? To live our dreams? To get out of the rat race?

Quit the Rat Race

What if, after some point in time, a creation of our own hard work can take over for us in continuing the livelihood for the rest of our lives and release us from the chains of the rat race? From that day, what if we don't have to worry about going to work for our monthly pay-checks or our yearly increments?

Is this possible?

My idea about work–life balance is very different from the conventional one. In the initial stages of our careers, there is a requirement to slog hard to finally reach a successful stage. We rarely get to pursue our areas of interest and our dreams through our careers. So, for most of us, it is work, work and work in that initial phase. It is only in the second phase of our lives that we begin to focus on our selves. We may, then, ask these questions to ourselves:

What is my area of interest? Where does my passion lie?

What would I like to do if the money factor wasn't the sole consideration? What do I want to do in the second half of my life? After all the hard work, this is the point where we shift our focus to our life. We start balancing the number of years of work with the number of years in life.

Is this possible?

Absolutely!

So, take a moment to answer these questions. Think about what you want in life and then figure out how much money at what points in life you need to make this happen.

Examples of goals are:

Short Term	Long Term
Take a vacation every year with your family	Pay for your child's higher education
Buy a car	Buy a house
Expenses for a wedding or other celebrations	Get a monthly income without working for it

This, by the way, is called goal-based planning and is a better approach to investing. It allows you to invest in a way that is aligned with what you want in life. Remember, the purpose of investing is not to hoard money but to live a life you desire. And that's what the goal-based approach allows you to do.

For example, goal-based planning helped me become insurance-free. At 30, when I had become a first-time dad, I wanted to build a corpus of ₹1 crore. The idea was that if something happens to me, my family will get ₹1 crore. I had assumed that I would be able to add ₹20 lakh to my corpus every five years. So, I took five term-life insurance policies of ₹20 lakh each with 5-, 10-, 15-, 20-, and 25-year maturity. The plan was that as I kept adding money to the corpus, I would keep letting the policies lapse, since I already had that amount. I didn't have to wait for 25 years, though. With a systematic approach, I was able to build ₹1 crore corpus in just seven years and cancel all the insurance policies. That ₹1 crore has, since then, grown to become a lot more. And now, I put the insurance premium to use and buy EMFs instead. The returns from my corpus are more than enough to meet any emergency needs. Moral of the story? Think through your goals and invest accordingly.

For the purpose of this book, your goal is financial freedom by 45. So, think through a bit about what financial freedom means to you. Think about how much money you will need every month to be able to relax about financial commitments. What is the amount you need to meet all your financial obligations when you retire? This could be a sum of your monthly expenses, a continuation of your current or expected future salary or any other parameter you choose to employ. And, don't forget to add inflation—take a thumb-rule of 5 per cent in yearly rise in prices.

Great! Now you have a number. All we need to do now is to build an investing discipline and methodology to get you to this number.

BUILDING AN INVESTING DISCIPLINE

Early in my career, it was a meeting of minds when I met my mentor Prashant Jain, one of the sharpest minds in the fund management business and a big follower and advocate of disciplined investing. He was heading the investments team of the boutique MF company that I joined in 2000, and went on to become the chief investment officer of one of the largest MF companies, creating a successful track record of managing funds for three decades. During one of my early interactions with him, he gave me some golden rules that have stuck with me forever:

'Spend *after* you invest from your monthly pay-check.'

'At the end of the month, if you have even a thousand rupees left in your bank account, invest it in the equity fund.'

These were lessons on starting to save early, spend within my means and follow a disciplined approach to investing that helped me.

Before we move any further, I want to emphasize a very important distinction. In this book, we are not *saving* for the future; we are *investing* in it. And there's a *big* difference between these two approaches.

Savings should be considered as just storing your money safely. It is what you put in fixed deposits, current and savings accounts. You store this money, but it stagnates. Your principal usually remains constant, but you earn some interest.

Investments are where you take some calculated risks and target higher returns with the objective of *growing your money*. It is what you make in stocks, property or units of EMFs.

Savings are for your short-term and emergency needs while investments are made to meet your long-term financial goals like retirement.

This book is about investing, and specifically, equity investing. And so, when we talk of building a discipline, it is about adding money to your equity investments regularly and systematically.

Why is discipline so important in equity investing? This is a way to overcome all those challenges that individual investors face while trying to invest in the stock market. Discipline helps you build healthy investing habits, and once ingrained, those habits save you from making the wrong decisions in times of market volatility. This actually reminds me of an interesting story from my school days.

La Martiniere College, Lucknow, my alma mater, is known for its traditions and its long history of inculcating discipline and integrity in its students since 1845. Many of our alumni have joined the armed forces and have done the country proud. A few years ago, a tablet was unveiled in our college hall in honour of all our decorated war heroes, recipients of Param Vir Chakra, Maha Vir Chakra and the Vir Chakra. It was a testament to the fact that we lived and breathed discipline, and our habits were hard to break.

On the first day of the session, when I was in Class 8, our English teacher Mr Carville, who was also the class teacher of our section, called for introductions. Now, it had been ingrained in us to address our teachers as 'sir' whenever we spoke to them. If we were answering a question, we would begin as, 'Sir, the answer is …'. So, the introductions started like this:

> Mr Carville points to Student A: 'Tell me your name.'
> Student A: 'Sir, Deepak Mullick.'
> Maybe Mr Carville wanted to test our manners or just wanted to lighten the mood of the class…
> Mr Carville: '*Sir* Deepak Mullick, we have a *knight* among us!'
> He then pointed to Student B: 'What's your name?'
> Student B: 'Sir, Anuranjan Bist'
> Mr Carville: '*Sir* Anuranjan Bist, another knight!'

The thing was, while we all laughed when student after student kept on uttering 'sir' before saying his own name, as a matter of discipline, nobody introduced himself without first addressing the teacher, and all 42 of us attained knighthood that day!

But humour aside, in my career, I have seen the power of investing discipline and the impact it can have on your financial well-being. And one of the best ways to inculcate this discipline is through SIPs.

TAMING THE VOLATILITY SYSTEMATICALLY

Each and every individual attempts to create predictability in every walk of life—predictability in their career path, personal relationships, health, security and predictability of finances to cover all their needs, present and future! But as they say, the only certainty about life is uncertainty. My approach is to help you tame this uncertainty.

Peter Lynch rightly said, 'Far more money has been lost by investors preparing for corrections, or trying to anticipate corrections, than has been lost in corrections themselves.'

My 25 years of experience in the investments industry has made me realize that a lot more people can take advantage of India's growth story in a simple way. Along with entrepreneurs, common people, too, can accumulate a decent amount of wealth and become financially independent by applying a simple technique of participation in the India growth story.

What if a person who started his career in 1994 began saving ₹1,800 monthly in a particular savings technique? What if this meagre investment of ₹1,800 a month continued for 25 years and resulted in the creation of a wealth of ₹1 crore?

On the contrary, what if someone who retired in 1994 with a retirement corpus of ₹1 crore applied the very same technique—not only fetching him a pension of ₹1 lakh per month but also growing his corpus from ₹1 crore to more than ₹14 crore in 25 years? That sounds too good to be true, right?

What if I told you that these are not any random hypothetical figures, but actual data of a commonly available investment vehicle? I'm talking about a systematic investment in MFs.

We talked about how it is difficult for individual investors to invest in the equity markets because they don't have the time or the resources needed to understand the dynamics at play. A great way to overcome this difficulty is to invest in equity-based MFs.

Mutual funds are managed by experienced fund managers backed by years of experience and resources to track the performance of companies the fund invests in. Mutual funds offer a much more transparent investment environment with a much better track record of building wealth because of their excellent stock-picking abilities. For example, let's take a look at the performance of two MFs—HDFC Flexi-cap Fund and ICICI Prudential Multicap Fund (see Tables 5 and 6). They have consistently outperformed the Sensex in 5-, 10-, and 15-year timeframes.

Table 5
Performance of HDFC Flexi-cap Fund in 5-, 10-, and 15-year timeframes

HDFC Flexi-cap Fund			Compounded Annually			
No.	Year-End	NAV	Returns 1 Yr	Returns 5 Yrs	Returns 10 Yrs	Returns 15 Yrs
0	Mar-95	9.09				
1	Mar-96	7.06	-22			
2	Mar-97	5.76	-18			
3	Mar-98	7.48	30			
4	Mar-99	12.62	69			
5	Mar-00	24.89	97	22		
6	Mar-01	16.44	-34	18		
7	Mar-02	22.31	36	31		
8	Mar-03	22.26	0	24		
9	Mar-04	51.6	132	33		
10	Mar-05	67.3	30	22	22	
11	Mar-06	127.15	89	51	34	
12	Mar-07	142.6	12	45	38	
13	Mar-08	165.79	16	49	36	
14	Mar-09	108.85	-34	16	24	
15	Mar-10	236.27	117	29	25	24
16	Mar-11	283.28	20	17	33	28
17	Mar-12	261.67	-8	13	28	29
18	Mar-13	271.11	4	10	28	27
19	Mar-14	331.99	22	25	20	24
20	Mar-15	469.72	41	15	21	22
21	Mar-16	416.7	-11	8	13	24
22	Mar-17	543.77	30	16	14	24

23	Mar-18	591.57	9	17	14	24
24	Mar-19	681.21	15	15	20	19
25	Mar-20	457.74	-33	-1	7	14
26	Mar-21	797.45	74	14	11	13
27	Mar-22	1011.3	27	13	14	14
28	Mar-23	1121.5	11	14	15	14
Probability of Gains			21 in 28	23 in 24	19 in 19	14 in 14

Source: Data collated and calculated from NAV data of the MF scheme and HDFC Mutual Fund Factsheet, March 2023.

Table 6
Performance of ICICI Prudential Multicap Fund in 5-, 10-, and 15-year timeframes

ICICI Pru Multicap Fund			Compounded Annually			
No.	Year-end	NAV	Returns 1 Yr	Returns 5 Yrs	Returns 10 Yrs	Returns 15 Yrs
0	Mar-95	10.34				
1	Mar-96	8.6	-17			
2	Mar-97	7.66	-11			
3	Mar-98	7.79	2			
4	Mar-99	9.44	21			
5	Mar-00	21.6	129	16		
6	Mar-01	10.22	-53	4		
7	Mar-02	11.94	17	9		
8	Mar-03	12.8	7	10		
9	Mar-04	28.11	120	24		
10	Mar-05	36.29	29	11	13	
11	Mar-06	69.16	91	47	23	
12	Mar-07	77.49	12	45	26	
13	Mar-08	87.93	13	47	27	

ICICI Pru Multicap Fund			Compounded Annually			
No.	Year-end	NAV	Returns 1 Yr	Returns 5 Yrs	Returns 10 Yrs	Returns 15 Yrs
14	Mar-09	55.36	-37	15	19	
15	Mar-10	102.94	86	23	17	17
16	Mar-11	115.89	13	11	27	19
17	Mar-12	105.63	-9	6	24	19
18	Mar-13	112.27	6	5	24	19
19	Mar-14	139.38	24	20	17	20
20	Mar-15	198.24	42	14	19	16
21	Mar-16	192.78	-3	11	11	22
22	Mar-17	254.78	32	19	13	23
23	Mar-18	269.19	6	19	12	23
24	Mar-19	295.61	10	16	18	17
25	Mar-20	206	-30	1	7	12
26	Mar-21	357.55	74	13	12	12
27	Mar-22	440.34	23	12	15	12
28	Mar-23	454.3	3	11	15	12
Probability of Gains			21 in 28	24 in 24	19 in 19	14 in 14

Source: Data collated and calculated from NAV data of the MF scheme and ICICI Prudential Mutual Fund Factsheet, March 2023.

In addition, MF norms on expenses, fees, distribution expenses, return assurance, advertisement, etc., are very strictly regulated by the Securities and Exchange Board of India (SEBI), the body responsible for regulating all capital markets of our country with investor-interest protection.

Starting SIPs in EMFs is the best way for individual investors to participate in India's growth story.

An SIP is a regular, fixed investment made towards an MF scheme. While the frequency of SIPs can vary, I recommend building a monthly SIP where even small amounts can get you large gains over the long term. Small and regular investments are a great way to build financial discipline and a corpus over time. But the best thing about SIPs is that *they eliminate the need to time the markets*. You don't need to know whether the market is doing well or going down. You just put in the same amount month after month and let the acquisition cost average out over time. It reduces the risk of making one large equity investment at one time.

That happens because SIPs follow this interesting technique of rupee cost averaging (RCA). When you invest a fixed amount at regular intervals, you end up buying more units when the prices are low and fewer units when the prices are high. And so, in the long term, you end up with a drastically low cost per unit of shares acquired (see Figure 5). And the longer you do this, the better the impact of RCA.

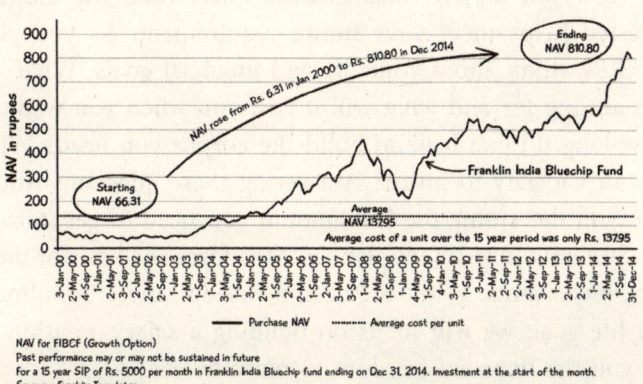

Figure 5: Cost per unit drops drastically over longer periods (assuming markets have moved up over this period)

Source: FT-20 SIPs Made Easy, Franklin Templeton Investments, February 2015.

If you see the example in the figure above for FI Bluechip Fund (Growth Option), for a person who invests through an SIP, the average cost per unit is ₹137.95. Let's say they invest ₹5,000 per month over 15 years, investing a total of ₹9 lakh.

Another person tries to time the markets and makes nine lump-sum investments of ₹1 lakh each, totalling the same ₹9 lakh. He ends up investing only during the 'good times' and invests all instalments closer to the peaks. Given the market and fund performance, his average cost per unit is ₹184.27, 34 per cent higher than that of the person who decided to invest in SIPs.

Even if your cash flows are such that you can only invest in lump sums, you can take advantage of RCA with systematic transfer plans (STPs). With an STP you can invest the lump-sum in a liquid, short-term debt instrument and then, over time, shift it in equal instalments to EMFs.

However, an SIP makes sense only when the amount invested helps meet your future requirement. As you plan for SIPs, think about your life and financial goals. What are you aiming for and what will it cost you when you want it? How long do you have to build the corpus you need? What is your capacity to invest? Answering these questions would help you determine the SIP amount you need to get started.

Systemic investment plans in MFs form the basis of the 1 per cent formula. While SIPs can be used to invest for almost any life goal, we will focus on building a salary–pension to get you the financial freedom to retire by 45!

But before we get started on the 1 per cent formula, let's dive deeper into the mindset that continues to drive investments in asset classes like real estate and gold that barely beat inflation and do nothing to create long-term wealth.

KEY TAKEAWAYS AND REFLECTIONS

1. To make money, mindset is more important than a degree in finance. If you are able to separate emotions from numbers and ride out the ups and downs of the market, you will win.
2. When it comes to investing in equity, do not operate from a place of greed or fear—think like a business owner and make practical, thought-through decisions. Perhaps the worst time to invest is when everyone is optimistic about the market!
3. Set your financial goals and take a disciplined approach to achieve them.
4. Rupee cost averaging is your friend. Make the most of it by starting SIPs in EMFs.

CHEW ON THIS

1. How do you think about money? How does it help or hinder you?
2. Are you clear about your financial goals?

5

Roti, Kapda and 2BHK

'*Get a job, get married, buy a house and then you'll be settled in life,*' says every Indian parent ever. How familiar are you with this dialogue? Have you wondered why buying a house is the epitome of being 'settled' in the Indian context?

'Buying my house was a dream come true!'

'I felt great when I was able to buy a house for my parents.'

'When my children grow up, I am going to leave them a house each.'

Real estate investments are deeply entrenched in our psyche. In another conversation with my friend Dr Bist, he said that it has to do with our colonial past. We have dealt with so much hardship and lived with the fear of everything being taken away that now we want to be assured of the tangibility of our assets. Buying a house is imprinted in our minds as a measure of stability and safety.

A house is real! Money in the bank or, heaven forbid, the stock market? That's just numbers! And numbers are not so reassuring, are they? A house doesn't fluctuate like a stock market index: it sits there strong and solid. And it's the same with gold. People hoard gold and consider buying jewellery as an investment!

The thought that drives it is that even if the prices don't go up and the return is nil, at least with a house or gold, you don't lose your original investment. This fear of loss is very real in a downturn in the stock market. When you see your wealth being wiped out, it's tough to sit tight and do nothing. Buying a house doesn't come with these bouts of anxiety. Once you've made it, it stays with you.

What you can see, feel and touch is real. It's reassuring. If it's in your hands, it's yours!

For the generations of our parents and grandparents who lived through Partition, for instance, a house was a big deal. It wasn't easy to buy or build a house. They didn't have access to the finances. They had to save almost all their lives to be able to afford their own house.

Compared to them, today, higher incomes, easy access to credit, payment schemes etc., make it possible for people in their 20s to buy a house. And because they can, parents also pressurize them to do it!

Having a tangible asset also tells the world about your worth—that you have 'made it' in life. People can see how big your house is, how much gold you wear and what car you drive. They can't see how many zeros there are in your bank account.

And we all love to brag, don't we?

No wonder Indians have 84 per cent of their wealth parked in real estate, 11 per cent in gold and just 5 per cent in financial assets. Even from that 5 per cent, 90 per cent of investments are in safe deposits like FDs, PPF and post office schemes that are considered more tangible than investments in equities.[1]

---

[1]Household Finance Committee, *Indian Household Finance*, RBI, July 2017.

But have you ever wondered what this obsession with tangibility and extreme safety is costing you?

Your life and your freedom!

Yes, you read that right.

By putting your money into real estate, you are wasting your most productive years paying EMIs instead of building wealth. A big chunk of what you earn goes into this capital guzzling, illiquid, depreciating asset. And when you retire, the returns from real estate (that is, rent) are not enough to sustain your income needs. Similarly for gold, it makes no sense to hoard it. Sure, buy some to wear. But keeping gold bars, gold coins and unnecessary jewellery in your locker is just locking away your financial freedom.

But, back to the bigger problem—the obsession with real estate! Let me tell you a story of two friends who experienced that. Aman and Vikas met each other in 2011 when they were 30 years old. They were moving into the same housing society with their families where they continued to stay for 12 years. They were from similar backgrounds, worked similar jobs and had shared interests, and so, from neighbours, they went on to become good friends. While they found many things in common, their approach to real estate was very different. While Vikas had bought the house he stayed in, Aman stayed in a rented place.

Vikas's house cost ₹45 lakh, and to pay for it, he had taken a 20-year loan of ₹40.5 lakh that he repaid at an EMI of ₹35,000 per month. He paid the rest of the ₹4.5 lakh from his existing savings. He also paid ₹3.6 lakh as registration and stamp duty. In addition, for the taxes and upkeep of the house, Vikas had to set aside ₹1,000 per month.

On the other hand, Aman's rent started out at ₹8,000 per

month and, over time, grew to ₹14,000 per month. For the 12 years that he stayed in the society, this averaged to about ₹11,000 per month. Given Aman's and Vikas's similar incomes, Aman also had a surplus of ₹25,000 per month left over, since he wasn't paying EMIs or property maintenance expenses like Vikas.

Aman used this ₹25,000 to invest in a monthly SIP in three EMF schemes. In addition, he also invested ₹8.1 lakh—an amount equal to what Vikas paid as down payment and registration fee for the house—as lump-sum investment in EMFs in the same year.

After 12 years, their family's needs had changed, and, with growing children, both needed bigger accommodation. Vikas decided to sell the existing house to fund the bigger house and wanted to see what his financial position was based on the investment he had made 12 years ago. Vikas heard market rumours that real estate prices have more than doubled since he bought the house, and he thought it's a great time to sell. However, when he actually started looking for buyers, he couldn't find anyone willing to pay that much. Finally, after months of effort and hassles with brokers, he was able to find a buyer at ₹85 lakh. With that amount, his financial position looked something like this:

SAVINGS MADE BY VIKAS AFTER 12 YEARS	
House sale price according to market rates	₹85,00,000
Brokerage and builder NOC charges	-1,20,000
Housing loan remaining	-24,20,000
Net savings	₹59,60,000

On the other hand, Aman's financial position painted a very different picture.

SAVINGS MADE BY AMAN AFTER 12 YEARS	
Mutual Fund Investments (HDFC Flexi-cap, Mirae Em. Bluechip and Franklin Ind. Focused in 2:2:1 proportion) • ₹25,000 per month SIP for 12 years • ₹8,10,000 lump-sum invested initially	₹1,53,76,198

With systematic investments in EMFs, his portfolio had grown to over ₹1.5 crore, almost three times of what Vikas had!

Albert Einstein famously said that compound interest is the most powerful force in the universe. His exact words were: 'Compound interest is the eighth wonder of the world. He who understands it, earns it; he who doesn't, pays it.' The initial years of our career are very conducive to investing in equities and understanding how the power of compounding works at its best. One can, of course, choose not to understand this powerful force and, instead, pay EMIs!

Buying a house, especially early on in life, is not a good financial decision. Not to mention all the other hassles that come with owning a house—you have to pay registration, property tax, spend more in case of property damage, pay for regular maintenance, etc. If you don't live in the house you buy, the rent is nowhere near the EMI you pay and you might even have to deal with unreasonable tenants who bother you for every little thing.

Real estate is also a risky investment if you don't do all the due diligence. You might end up buying a property that is disputed or doesn't have all the legal clearances. Builders might make false promises to make the project more lucrative.

And even if you do the due diligence, factors that would have increased the value of the property such as metro connectivity, airports, IT parks might end up getting reconsidered. And if you've watched the movie *Khosla ka Ghosla*, you know that real estate also comes with the risk of illegal occupation, land grabs, etc.—hassles we can all live without!

Even with these factors, we continue to chase the dream of owning our own house, chasing a generational idea and killing our future wealth and retirement lifestyle.

The Story of the Common Woman

Rahul's father, Mr J.N. Gupta, was a man of principles. He believed that a person is nothing if he doesn't believe in his principles. After a four-decade career in the FMCG sector, at the ripe age of 60, he retired as the general manager of Time Soaps and Detergents Pvt. Ltd. Post retirement, life in his hometown Dehradun had changed. What used to be a small, sleepy town for retirees, after becoming Uttarakhand's capital, had transformed into a mini metro. Living expenses had shot through the roof. Mr Gupta was finding it a little difficult to manage with the returns from all his investments but felt too embarrassed to ask for any assistance from his only child.

Three years ago, he had suffered a mild stroke and, since then, had been bed-ridden with some old-age ailment or the other. Back then, Rahul, along with his pregnant wife Sanjana and five-year-old daughter Sanya, had come over from Delhi for the Diwali holidays. The time had been appropriate to pass on some financial wisdom that a father had accumulated over his lifespan to his son.

'Never be under the burden of a loan!'

'Never ever invest in shares—it is gambling!'

Rahul was a hard-working man; like his father, he also believed in being principled. His public-school education and humble upbringing had taught him important life lessons. Having to search for a living in Delhi had made him a little more practical in life than his father. He would never let his ego come in between his boss's demands and commands, and he smartly worked his way up the corporate ladder. He had become the youngest regional sales manager at Unitelekom Ltd., one of the largest players in the Telecom industry in the country, earning a cool ₹24 lakh salary per annum just seven years into his career. Rahul always dreamt big and strived hard to fulfil those dreams. His wife Sanjana was his MBA batch mate, and she, too, came from a similarly humble background, but together, they had big aspirations for themselves and their children.

Rahul's company had an annual off-site visit for senior management staff in London. This year the company made an exception to invite their highest-ever target-achieving regional sales manager to the off-site as a gesture of appreciation. Rahul was simply ecstatic. It was the first time that he had travelled outside the country and that too—straight to the beautiful city of London! He wished he could bring his family here someday... All the sleepless nights dealing with unprofessional channel partners and the struggle to keep spirits high within his young and underpaid sales team were finally paying off. The big highlight of the off-site was the lecture given by Dr T. Albright, a special invitee from the faculty of the London School of Economics. Rahul was very impressed by Dr Albright's talk, his clarity of thought and the finesse with which he communicated the points across. His mind drew immediate comparisons with the faculty back home in the university from where he had graduated. That is when he decided to send Sanya abroad for her graduation.

'What I could not even dream for myself, I would get for my children,' he thought.

Sanjana was also extremely happy. She was very proud of all of Rahul's achievements in his career. Initially, she had felt guilty for not being able to support the family income after she had to leave her job for two years due to a difficult pregnancy. Now things were looking up, and she was happy to give the much-required moral support to a stressful career for her husband, with her not wanting him to worry about matters of the home. Both her parents were in government jobs, and she always missed having her mother to talk to. She did not want Sanya to feel the same void during her childhood.

Another longing she had from her childhood, after witnessing her parents go through nine transfers from place to place, was to have a house that she could call her own.

But even though they saved and curbed expenses, the money never seemed enough for all their dreams. Finally, after managing to save ₹20 lakh, they took a loan of ₹30 lakh and bought a house for ₹50 lakh. Rahul's take-home salary was ₹1.3 lakh, and their monthly expenses were just under ₹1 lakh. This decision to buy a house wiped out their savings and added a monthly EMI burden of ₹30,000. This left them nothing for emergencies and no leeway to even save or invest for the other dreams they had for themselves and their children.

If, on the other hand, Rahul and Sanjana had chosen to invest their savings and EMI amount into EMFs, after five years, their corpus would have been about ₹60 lakh (at 12 per cent compounding). That would have paid for the house without the need for a massive loan. In 10 years, this amount would have been over ₹1.31 crore—enough to take care of all their dreams!

> Buying a house to call it home is every Indian's dream, but there is a right time to do that. When one has to give up all that one has saved and then commit to EMIs that restrict the ability to save for many more years to come, it is definitely a huge mistake!

REAL ESTATE: A PLACE TO LIVE OR AN INVESTMENT?

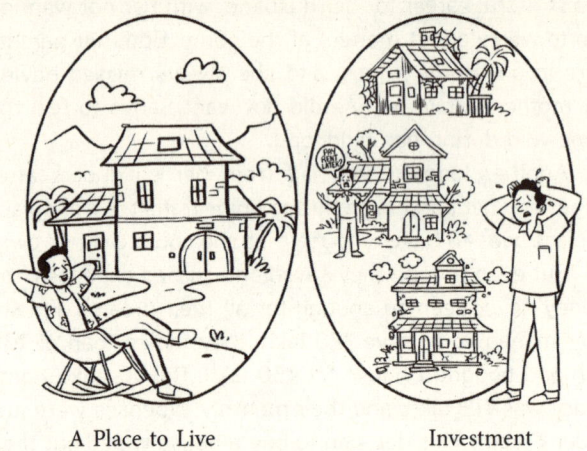

A Place to Live   Investment

Real Estate

You might be thinking that if no one builds or buys houses, where will people live? After all, everyone needs a roof over their head, right? Yes, they do! And so, before I move ahead in my argument against investing a large amount of savings in real estate, I would like to clear the distinction between a *consumer* of real estate and an *investor* in real estate.

The one house you purchase to live in is certainly not an investment. If you have the privilege, building a retirement home in your hometown or even a small holiday home or farmhouse for personal consumption may not be counted as an investment (provided you have substantial investments other than real estate). Anything beyond personal consumption, where people purchase real estate to sell in the future to make profits, is what we consider an investment in real estate.

But even if you are buying a house for your own consumption, it's a better idea financially to buy it later in life.

Let's go back to Vikas and see how his financial position would have changed if he delayed his decision to buy a house. If instead of buying a house in 2011 when he was 30 years old, he invested the money in EMFs like Aman, by 2023 (when he was 42), Vikas would also have a corpus of over ₹1.5 crore. This stronger financial situation would have made it easier for him to buy a house without eroding this wealth.

WHY INVESTING IN REAL ESTATE (OR GOLD) IS A BAD IDEA

The parent company of the organization that I worked for is the biggest supplier of home loans in India. Its job is to keep track of trends in the demand for homes across segments, home prices and affordability at each segment of the Indian household.

During my tenure there, I had a very interesting conversation with a veteran colleague, which helped me understand an important dynamic of the sector and forever changed my view on real estate.

This was in 2008, the year we witnessed the unfolding of the global financial crisis. There had been a long cycle of demand-led price spurt for homes and prices of real estate had risen manifold. This had continued for a good 10–12 years and, along with the real estate development sector, all ancillary sectors even remotely related to construction were booming. Real estate has become *the* buzzword in all my social circles, and everyone was talking about how it was the only investment avenue to get rich quickly!

As my colleague and I spoke about the positive sentiment around real estate, I could tell there was something bothering him. Our parent company was making big profits, creating massive wealth for our colleagues who had ESOP grants, yet, he seemed skittish about the immediate future of the industry.

When I prodded him about it, he opened up. Here's what was bothering him:

> You see, India's growth story has always been defined by the big multiplier effect that the large number of middle-income households create. The rich, even at high affordability levels, are so few in number that they do not add up to anything substantial in overall sales figures.

And here he said lies the challenge for real estate. 'The bulk of the demand for homes comes from the middle-income households where the affordability is below ₹40 lakh. But availability of real estate, the bulk supply, is at the ₹1 crore plus level.'

'It's a bubble,' he said.

And a bubble it was.

In 2009, the sub-prime crisis in the US (another crisis led by real estate price bubble burst) snowballed into the global financial crisis, and the real estate sector in India crashed and came to a standstill. Many projects failed to deliver, so many developers, including some big names, announced bankruptcy, and several malpractices and fraudulent activities were unearthed by authorities.

This down cycle has lasted for 10–12 years, and it is not until recent times, when affordable housing catering to end-user demand has become the buzzword, that the sector is reviving.

But does that mean you should invest in real estate? No, not really.

Real estate investors operate on a fallacy—that the cycle of high demand, rising prices, will continue forever.

- They forget that houses are meant for end users who would eventually make it their home and live in it.
- They forget that the property that they purchase is subject to wear and tear and is a depreciating asset.
- They forget that eventually, it is the affordability factor that will reign supreme and the government of the day, present or future, will always encourage an environment of low prices till a majority of households have their own homes.

As governments focus on making housing more affordable, and the increase in cost of building real estate is linked to inflation, it follows that the increase in price of finished houses is also linked to inflation. This means that returns from investments in real estate will also be linked to inflation. And we are not even considering tax, or the depreciation for wear and tear, or location disadvantage arising out of infrastructure development, and not adjusting for any expenses that have been incurred in the upkeep of the property!

If you look back at Vikas's example, his purchase cost of the house in 2011 was ₹45 lakh. When he sold the house

12 years later, he only managed to get ₹85 lakh for it. That's just 5.44% CAGR—approximately equal to the inflation in the last 12 years (2011–23). Once you add the expenses towards loan interest, maintenance, taxes, brokerage, and builder no objection certificate (NOC) charges, the returns are much less!

So what happens to all that money you put into buying that second or third house? It has barely kept up with inflation, leaving you much worse off than what you would have been if you had chosen to put your hard earned money in a financial instrument.

It's the same story with gold. During my time in Delhi for a work-related role, one of our neighbours, Krishnans, came from very traditional South Indian business family background. Though we had little in common, our children going to the same playschool soon made us great family friends. I left Delhi after four years, and though we stopped being neighbours, we kept in touch.

Soon after our move into our flat in 2003, they were blessed with a baby girl in March. On the twelfth day of her birth, we were invited to a very elaborate naming ceremony at their house. As was tradition in their family, the new mother's parents gifted their granddaughter with 1 kg gold. 'This will help baby Ramya when she gets married,' they said.

By the time Ramya was finishing school in 2021, marriage was the last thing on her mind. She had been born and brought up in a metro city with the modern Gen Z thought process. She dreamt of a foreign education and, after that, a good career to make her an independent woman.

In one of our conversations, Ramya's father had shared with me his inability to fund the high cost of a foreign undergraduate degree. His business had suffered badly during the Covid days and he had exhausted all of his savings to get the business running again. He had considered selling off the gold that her grandmother had given during her birth and yet the money was not adding up.

Here's how much the gold gifted to Ramya had grown in value:

Cost of 10 g gold on 31 March 2003 = ₹5,332
Cost of 1 kg gold on 31 March 2003 = ₹5.332 lakh
Cost of 10 g gold on 31 March 2021 = ₹44,648
Cost of 1 kg gold on 31 March 2021 = ₹44.648 lakh
So Ramya had accumulated around ₹45 lakh in 18 years!

Let's see what would have happened if, instead of gold, Ramya's grandparents had given her an investment in EMFs.

NAV of HDFC Flexi-cap fund on 31 March 2003 = ₹22.26 per share
Units purchased with an investment of ₹5.332 lakh = 23,953.279 units
NAV of HDFC Flexi-cap fund on 31 March 2021 = ₹797.451 per share
NAV of 23,953.279 units of HDFC Flexi-cap Fund on 31 March 2021 = ₹1.91 crore

Good enough for a four-year undergraduate course in the US!

In fact, if you really study the numbers, you'll see that gold has barely beaten inflation all these years. In a period from 1980 to 2023, the CAGR returns from gold have been 8.90 per cent whereas the average inflation has been 7.63 per cent.[2]

---

[2] Calculated on the basis of data available from Bloomberg, *RBI Handbook of Statistics on Indian Economy*, National Savings Institute and State Bank of India (for details, see 'Asset class comparison' in this chapter).

So that's just 1–2 per cent more than inflation.

NOT ALL FINANCIAL ASSETS GIVE EQUAL RETURNS

If you are thinking that your money is safe from the fallacy of investing in tangible assets because you haven't invested in gold and real estate, think again!

Even if your money is invested in a financial instrument, it might not be generating the returns you want.

As we saw earlier, only 5 per cent of the wealth in Indian households is invested in financial assets. Even from this meagre proportion, 53 per cent is held in bank deposits; 24 per cent in life insurance funds; 13 per cent in currency; and around 10 per cent in MFs. Of this 10 per cent, half of the investments are in debt-oriented MF schemes.

Figure 6 demonstrates how these assets perform against inflation: if you look at the average inflation from 1980 to 2023, it's around 7.63 per cent. And here is how the CAGR of various asset classes measures up against inflation.

- Bank FD = Inflation + 0.5–1 per cent
- Small savings (PF/PPF/Post Office) = Inflation + 1–2 per cent
- Equities = Inflation + 7–8 per cent

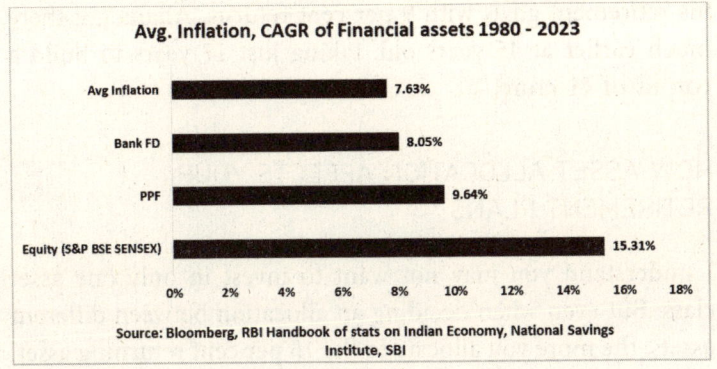

Figure 6: Asset class comparison

Source: Bloomberg, *RBI Handbook of Statistics on Indian Economy*, National Savings Institute and State Bank of India.

Data clearly shows that one of the most neglected investment instruments—equities—is the one that has resulted in the highest, inflation-beating returns, while the assets Indians usually prefer to invest in are barely beating inflation and definitely not building long-term wealth!

Let's see how this choice of investing in an asset class that gives a return of 9 per cent versus one that gives 15 per cent affects our financial objectives.

Avik and Ahana were 28 years old and both had monthly savings of ₹10,000 each. They wanted to retire with a corpus of ₹1 crore. Avik distributed his savings to invest in gold, bank FDs and small savings that gave him a 9 per cent return. Ahana, on the other hand, started an SIP in equities that gave her a 15 per cent return. Guess at what age were they able to meet their retirement goals?

It took Avik almost 24 years (at 52 years old) to meet

his retirement goals with 9 per cent returns. Ahana got there much earlier at 45 years old, taking just 17 years to build a corpus of ₹1 crore.

HOW ASSET ALLOCATION AFFECTS YOUR RETIREMENT PLANS

I understand you may not want to invest in only one asset class. But even when deciding an allocation between different assets, the more you allocate to the 15 per cent returning asset, the smaller the savings requirements will be and the lesser time it will take to accumulate a targeted corpus. Currently 99 per cent of Indian households' accumulated savings are in tangible assets or the safest-intangible financial instruments, and it is eroding your wealth.

There is a lot of debate about the benefits of asset allocation and diversification across multiple asset classes. I have a very different perspective on this. I believe that it is just a matter of carefully breaking down your requirements in the short-term and long-term buckets.

For your short-term needs, say up to two years of all your estimated expenses, the important thing is not the returns but the safety and liquidity of funds. So, this amount should be saved/stored in a stable asset class. However, for your long-term financial objectives (like achieving financial independence in 15–20 years), you should have lesser consideration for short-term stability and more towards long-term returns.

This is especially important if you are just starting out your career. That's a crucial point to start building long-term wealth. Don't waste these years in overthinking the short-term stability needs. In your 20s and 30s, your focus should be on the long term as your employment would provide for the short-term needs. Closer to retirement is when you should start preparing for the two-year stability bucket. This is also the time when the salaried people get their accumulated PF balance and retiral that are good enough for that requirement.

Despite the math clearly favouring long-term investments in the early years, people tend to think short term and allocate a higher percentage of savings in lower return assets. That just makes it harder to achieve retirement goals and takes so much longer! And that's why many people find it difficult to leave the shackles of the monthly salary and retire early. At the end of the day, often when it's too late, people realize that the safety-factor in these asset classes comes at a big cost.

Now that I have made you stop and think about where you are putting your money and how it's stopping you from building wealth, let's see how the 1 per cent formula can actually help you acquire what you desire, live a quality life *and* still leave more than enough to sustain your retirement.

KEY TAKEAWAYS AND REFLECTIONS

1. Everyone aspires to own a home to live in. By all means, buy a house, but as a place to live and not as an investment.
2. If you are buying a house, do so later in life, when your financial position is stronger and you have built a sustainable corpus.
3. Learn the difference between a real-estate consumer and investor.
4. Understand that you may only get returns from real-estate that keep pace with inflation but don't leave you with anything else but a roof over your head.

5. Don't invest in assets that are inflation-matching; rather, choose an inflation-beating strategy.

CHEW ON THIS

1. What is your motivation to invest in real estate?
2. Are you sure that this is the right asset class to meet your financial goals?
3. Is there a way we could turn volatility in our favour? Or reduce the volatility in equity markets? Is there a way where we don't have to worry about the volatility at all and still get the benefits of equity investing?

6

The 1 per cent Formula to Financial Freedom

Imagine that you live in a town where the water supply is inconsistent. You never know when the water will come or for how long or whether it's even going to be sufficient for the day's needs. What would you do in that case?

You'll build a reservoir tank that can store surplus water when available, and then use that collected water when there is water scarcity. But to make sure that the reservoir never runs out of water (as long as you stay within a reasonable limit of what you are using), you need to build it to a certain holding capacity and fill it up.

If you plan it right, then no matter how inconsistent the water supply is, you'll always have the water you need.

It's the same with money!

The town with water supply inconsistency is your retirement, where you may or may not have any income coming in. To ensure a steady water supply, that is, monthly income after retirement, you need a reservoir tank, that is, a corpus of funds that you can withdraw from. You build this reservoir during your working years, when you do have consistent income coming in every month. And you build it with SIPs in EMFs.

The size of the tank is the corpus you need to retire with.

But periods of drought are a real possibility in water scarce areas. When there is a drought, the reservoir tank may not be enough. So you need to consider some extra capacity in your tank when you decide on the size to tide you over in these tough times.

In monetary terms, this extra capacity is your volatility buffer. This is the cushion you build to account for any volatility in the market.

Once you have the appropriate reservoir capacity in place, you can take out 1 per cent of the corpus every month, without worrying about the inconsistencies in income or volatility in the market. And this is what the 1 per cent formula is all about.

If you have been hesitating to invest in equity markets because of their inherent volatility, this approach helps you take advantage of that volatility.

Simply put, the 1 per cent formula is an approach to build a corpus over 15 years that would give you a sustained salary-pension after this time period that amounts to 1 per cent of the original corpus. So, if you want a salary pension of ₹1 lakh per month after you are 45, you need to build a corpus of ₹1 crore by the time you are 42. I've added the extra three years to create your volatility buffer and an emergency corpus—something we'll talk about in a bit.

Does that sound a lot? What if I told you that it isn't that difficult? In fact, it is very easy to get to a ₹1 crore corpus and can be done with sustained SIP investments of just a few thousand rupees every month. The difficulty is in maintaining that financial discipline for those 15 years and staying put if there is volatility.

Are you wondering why 15 years? Well, you can even

build a corpus much faster than that, but this time frame is not without its importance. Stock market movements make sense only in the long-term, and to reach that understanding, you need to pass the short-term volatility test where the upswings and the crashes can defy all logic. In a 15-year period, you would have experienced one-to-two such market cycles. Talking about slumps and living through them are very different experiences. Actually, witnessing a market bounce back after a crash will give you the resilience required to stay invested. So ideally, a 15-year time frame is the perfect setting for the 1 per cent formula to work.

THE SALARY–PENSION

The idea behind the salary–pension is that we create a stream of monthly cash flow out of returns from investments in EMFs. Over time, the returns delivered will exceed the percentage of withdrawals, leaving a portion of the corpus to also grow with time. And the data from the past three decades support this.

Figure 7 shows the value of an investment of ₹1 crore over 29 years with monthly withdrawals of ₹1 lakh every month from the very first month after investing. Despite the withdrawals and market volatility, the value of the investment continues to grow significantly.

This is not a work of fiction but derived from data-backed analysis. The only assumption is the initial investment of ₹1 crore, and the rest is based on facts and figures taken from the NAV data of HDFC Balanced Advantage Fund, one of the most popular equity-oriented MF schemes in India.[1]

---

[1] This was one of the best performing schemes in the segment, and other

102 • *Gain Your Financial Freedom with the 1% Formula*

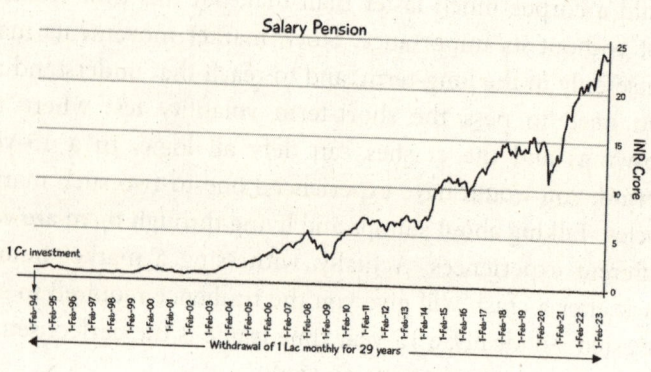

Figure 7: The golden goose

Source: Data calculated from NAV data of HDFC Balanced Advantage Fund

How is that for an early retirement when you are 45!

But most of the time, individual investors are unable to do this as the returns from stock markets are not linear. There are years of negative returns followed by some good years that make up for the entire period. The volatility dissuades people, and they remain stuck with low-return investments.

For the 1 per cent formula to work, you need to:

1. Create a 'salary–pension' corpus worth 100 times your monthly requirements in EMFs

---

schemes in the same time period may not show the same resilience. However, I have accounted for the fact that not all schemes are equal in the 1 per cent formula. In this book, we will look at building cushions and buffers for multiple types of schemes and scenarios to make the 1 per cent formula viable.

Stage 1

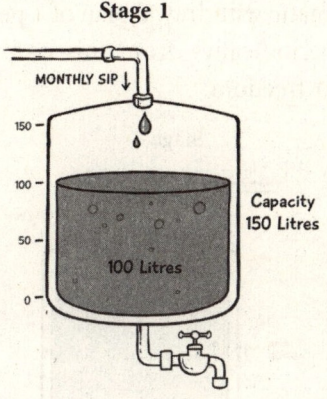

2. Wait three years for the corpus to stabilize and act as a 'volatility buffer' to 'cushion' for market cycles. In these three years, create an emergency corpus—worth two years of your monthly expenses—in a stable instrument like bank FD to add a further layer of cushioning against market risk.

Stage 2

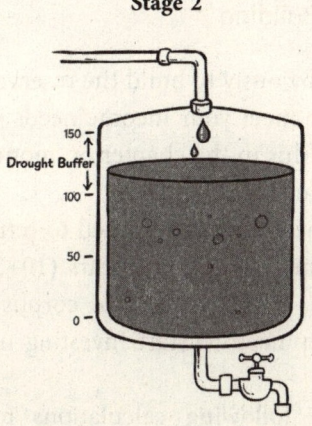

3. Start a systematic withdrawal plan of 1 per cent monthly—increasing periodically—from this corpus, which allows you financial freedom.

Stage 3

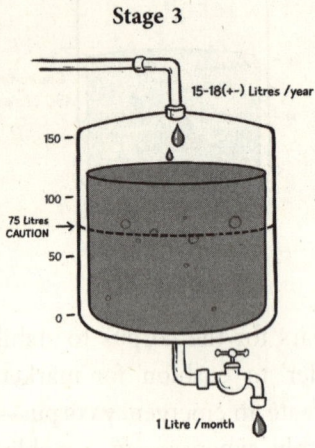

Let's take a look at how that works.

Stage 1: Corpus Building

The first stage is obviously to build the reservoir or the corpus that is sufficient to meet your income needs when you retire. We touched upon this in the chapter on money mindset. Let's now take some time to quantify it.

A couple in their early 30s wanted to retire by their mid-40s, which gave them around 13 years (10+3) to build their retirement corpus. What would that corpus look like? And how much do they need to start investing now to reach the target amount?

We used the following calculations to arrive at the numbers:

- We first totalled their monthly expenses—rent, house help, groceries, entertainment, etc.
- Then we added up expenses that come up annually, such as travel, insurance payments, maintenance, etc.
- We also added some expenses that they foresaw coming in the next five years.

At the present moment, these expenses for this couple were totalling up to about ₹1.5 lakh per month. So, the next step was to adjust this number for inflation and see what the total would be 13 years from now. Taking inflation at 5 per cent per annum, the total monthly expense when the couple planned to retire was ₹2.83 lakh per month.

As I mentioned earlier, the corpus should be 100 times the monthly expenses. Hence, the target corpus value for the couple was ₹2.83 crore. Let's see the breakdown of these numbers below.

Sample sheet to calculate target corpus as per expenses			
Monthly expenses			
Salaries of house help, cook, driver, gym instructor, etc.			₹35,000
Rent			₹35,000
Groceries			₹6,000
Eating out/ordering-in			₹7,500
Fuel, taxi, etc.			₹4,000
House maintenance, electricity, Internet, streaming services, water bill			₹11,000
Clothes, online shopping, splurging			₹10,000
		Sub-Total	₹1,08,500

Yearly expenses			
Yearly travel budget		₹75,000	
Car insurance and maintenance		₹15,000	
Festivals and occasions		₹20,000	
Son's school fees		₹2,50,000	
Extra/unexpected expenses		₹25,000	
		Sub-Total ₹3,85,000	
	Divide sub-total by 12 to get a monthly amount		₹32,083
5-yearly expenses			
House renovation		₹80,000	
Car Upgrade		₹5,00,000	
		Sub-Total ₹5,80,000	
	Divide this amount by 60 to get a monthly amount		₹9,667
Grand total			₹1,50,250
Grand total adjusted for inflation for future 10+3 years (5% p.a.)			₹2,83,000
Corpus Required = 100 x grand total			₹2.83 crore

The couple had been investing on and off in EMFs and presently had a corpus of ₹26 lakh. With this as the lump-sum, to reach ₹2.83 crore in 10+3 years, they would need to do an SIP of ₹65,000 monthly for the first five years. Then they would need to double this SIP to ₹1.3 lakh per month for the next five years. And finally, they need to let the corpus sit for three years.

Depending on any lump-sum amount you have available and the number of years you have till you need the salary-pension started, you can calculate the monthly investments you'll need to build your corpus. You can use the salary pension corpus calculator at www.simplymutual.com to find out the SIP you need to get started. As your earning potential grows, the SIP amount can increase too, creating the corpus faster. Also, with growing income and improving lifestyles, the levels of expenses may also go up, so go back to the calculations periodically to increase your target corpus and SIP amounts commensurately!

Recommended % of take-home income to go to SIPs in EMFs			
Age: 27–31	Age: 32–36	Age: 37–41	Age: 42+
Early Career Stage	Mid-Career Stage	Senior Career Stage	Financial Independence Stage nears
10–20%	20–30%	Greater than 30%, no upper limit	Continue same % to create emergency corpus

Angad, Ananya and Rohan were childhood friends who just turned 27. They had all passed out of college a few years ago and are now well settled in their jobs. Rohan just got married, and Angad and Ananya also plan to tie the knot with their respective partners and start their families in the next couple of years. Their saving capacity was 10–20 per cent of their take-home salary, and they wanted to start their investment journey for the future. At present, their focus was to save for a house, and over the next few years, they would also start thinking about a nest egg and for their kids' higher education.

Here's what their investment journey would look like over various stages of life.

Angad started investing with a monthly SIP of ₹20,000

	Age: 27-31		Age: 32-36		Age: 37-41		Age: 42
	Life Stage: Job, Marriage, Having Kids		Life Stage: Kids Reaching Senior School		Life Stage: Planning for Passion Pursuits		Salary-Pension Corpus Completed
	Starting SIP Amt		Nest Egg	New SIP Amt	Nest Egg	New SIP Amt	Nest Egg
Angad	₹20,000		₹1,649,727	₹40,000	₹62,06,837	₹80,000	₹1,75,37,477
Ananya	₹10,000		₹8,16,697	₹20,000	₹31,17,084	₹40,000	₹89,29,582
Rohan	₹5,000		₹4,08,348	₹10,000	₹15,58,542	₹20,000	₹44,64,791
	At 12% compounded monthly						

that created a corpus of over ₹16 lakh for him over five years. When he was 32, he doubled the SIP amount to ₹40,000. Over five years, his corpus grew to over ₹62 lakh. When he was 37, he doubled his SIP again and started investing ₹80,000 monthly. He stopped the SIPs in this corpus when he was 42. By that time, his corpus had grown to over ₹1.75 crore. After the cushion period, this would be ready to give him a steady salary–pension of ₹1.75 lakh per month!

Ananya and Rohan also started their investments at the same time. However, their starting SIPs were different from Angad. Ananya started with a ₹10,000 monthly SIP and Rohan started with ₹5,000 a month. Like Angad, they doubled their SIP amount every five years. By the time they turned 42, Ananya's corpus was close to ₹90 lakh, and Rohan's was around ₹45 lakh.

Let's do a quick activity now to see what your corpus could be in the 15-year time frame if you start today. Use the salary pension corpus calculator at www.simplymutual.com and make your own table. Try different combinations of the lump-sum and SIP amount to see the effect it has on your final corpus. The more you invest and stay invested, the bigger the returns.

However, to meet their life goals such as buying a house, paying for education, and so on, people do dip into their investments, and that can affect the final amount available to them for a salary–pension.

The following calculations show the final corpus for Angad over 15 years if he had withdrawn from it to pay for the down-payment of a house or for higher education. Even though the SIP amounts stay consistent, withdrawals lead to a significant drop in the final corpus value.

	Age: 27–31	Age: 32–36			Age: 37–41			Age: 42
	Life Stage: Job, Marriage, Having Kids	Life Stage: Kids Reaching Senior School			Life Stage: Planning for Passion Pursuits			Salary-Pension Corpus Completed
	Starting SIP Amt	Withdrawn	Nest Egg	New SIP Amt	Withdrawn	Nest Egg	New SIP Amt	Nest egg
No Withdrawal	₹20,000	0	₹16,49,727	₹40,000		₹62,06,837	₹80,000	₹1,75,37,477
House	₹20,000	₹16,49,727	0	₹40,000	₹1500000	₹32,99,455	₹80,000	₹1,24,13,676
House + Education	₹20,000	₹16,49,727	0	₹4,0000	₹1500000	₹17,99,455	₹80,000	₹97,79,164
				At 12% compounded monthly				

Some of these expenses like education are unavoidable, but we can be smarter when it comes to others like buying a house.

In Table 7, we see SIP returns of several funds since their inception and in the last 15 years. We can also see the monthly SIP amount it took in each fund to create a corpus of ₹1 crore in both time frames.

Table 7

SIP inception and 15-year returns

Scheme	Years since Inception	SIP since Inception		SIP over Last 15 Years	
		Returns	Monthly SIP Amt to Create ₹1 Crore	Returns	Monthly SIP Amt to Create ₹1 Crore
FI Bluechip	29.3	15.15%	₹1,900	11.00%	₹22,890
HDFC Bal Adv	29.2	18.37%	₹1,030	13.94%	₹17,780
FI Flexi-cap	28.5	19.18%	₹1,000	13.84%	₹17,950
HDFC Flexi-cap	28.3	20.39%	₹820	14.35%	₹17,170
HDFC Top100	26.5	18.02%	₹1,720	12.51%	₹20,120
DSP Flexi-cap	26	17.49%	₹2,050	12.57%	₹20,010
DSP Equity Opp	22.9	17.47%	₹3,420	13.62%	₹18,290
Kotak Bluechip	20.2	14.10%	₹8,220	12.10%	₹20,840
SBI Focused Eq	18.5	15.09%	₹9,230	15.62%	₹15,370
SBI Flexi-cap	17.6	12.12%	₹14,650	13.09%	₹19,130
FI Focused Eq	15.8	15.10%	₹14,270	15.56%	₹15,450
Mirae Largecap*	14.8	15.05%	₹16,600	15.05%	₹16,600

*15-year returns are actually for 14.8 years (inception). All returns data as on 31 March 2023.

Source: Data collated and calculated from the 2023 factsheet of the mentioned MFs.

Remember, in 'Decoding the Share Markets', we had seen the current (2023) Sensex 15-year CAGR at a multi-year low of 9 per cent as it reflected the impact of two large economy-slowing events: the global financial crisis post 2008 and the recent Covid-19 crisis. These recessionary periods reflect in the 15-year SIP returns of funds shown in the above table as well.

But what we learn from the table is that even in the worst of time periods, SIPs in EMFs can beat the index, and by maintaining the discipline of our monthly SIPs, amounts of ₹15,000–₹20,000 in 15 years can add up to a crore!

Stage 2: Volatility Buffer

The next stage is to protect your corpus from volatility and create that reserve tank capacity that will tide you over in rough times. Basically, this just means waiting three years for the corpus to stabilize.

Given the volatile nature of the markets, this volatility buffer, worth three years of market returns, is a fail-safe against market cycles built into the 1 per cent formula. The returns accruing into the corpus in these three years will act like a buffer for future volatile periods. At times, it may make your corpus grow in value, at other times, it will help bring the corpus to better valuations, but mostly it will be a mix of both—better value and better valuations.

For example, let's say you stopped adding to the corpus in year 15 from the date of your first SIP. Let's say, at this time, the market was at the peak of an irrational cycle of exuberance. This means that over the next few years, the market will see a correction and your corpus value will see a drop and then stabilize. If you also withdraw 1 per cent from it during this time, it may drop considerably and may not recover its original value. The volatility buffer helps prevent this. And if, by chance, you stop investing when the markets are low, your corpus would see a significant boost in this three-year waiting period when the markets rise again.

However, aside from your salary–pension corpus and volatility buffer, you also need an emergency fund in a fixed return instrument like a bank FD. This emergency fund should be worth two years of your expenses.

You can build this emergency fund by continuing your monthly investments in the three-year waiting period into a different instrument. This fund can be used in case of emergencies to avoid withdrawing lump-sums from your main corpus. You can also use this fund when, in case of short-term market volatility, your salary–pension fund drops 25 per cent from its original value. If you continue withdrawing from the corpus when it significantly drops in value, you end up eating into your principal. In this case, you should stop withdrawing the 1 per cent from your salary–pension fund and instead take it out from the emergency fund. This is again a mechanism that will help keep your salary–pension fund resilient in the face of market volatility.

This, in fact, happened to me. I retired when I was 42, and I was 100 per cent invested in EMFs. In the next two months, the market fell by 30 per cent. Luckily, my PF withdrawal money got credited in the bank at the same time, which I could use instead, to tide over for the next 12 months.

We talked about how I replaced my term-life insurance policies with my salary–pension corpus. Similarly, the emergency corpus could also replace your medical insurance policies.

A point to note is that when it comes to the emergency corpus, if you have withdrawn from it, then take care to replenish it as well. This can be done by withdrawing a bit extra from your salary–pension corpus once it has bounced back.

THE VIABILITY OF THE 1% FORMULA

I collated the NAV data since the inception of two schemes each for 10 of the top 15 MF companies in the country. I then examined this data for scenarios at different points of time where investors could start withdrawing from their corpus and came up with worst-case scenarios where there was a sharp fall or a long period of lull in the markets and the impact it would have on the corpus given the fact that we continue to withdraw 1 per cent monthly. While I analysed the data for all the crashes caused by national or international events in the last 25 or so years, two time periods stood out as being the worst of times:

1. The time immediately after the dot-com peak in early 2000 when the markets crashed
2. The time period from the peak (end 2007) just before the US sub-prime crisis snowballed into the global financial crisis

I, then, crunched the numbers to see how an investor's corpus performs with and without a three-year buffer and two-year emergency fund. It was clear that the required volatility buffer made it much more viable to maintain the salary–pension corpus even in the worst of the market cycles.

In Table 8, you can see how this pans out across time

Table 8
Feasibility of the 1 per cent formula considering worst-case scenarios

Scheme (Initial Corpus ₹1 crore)	Retirement Start Point (Event(S) That Followed)	Withdrawal Period Start Point	3-Year Cushion Period	Dip Into Emergency Corpus	Value of Corpus on 31 March 2023	Withdrawals till 31 March 2023
HDFC Balanced Adv	February 1994 (IPO scam, US sanctions, Kargil War)	Mar-94	No	No	₹23.39 crore	₹3.49 crore
ICICI Pru Large & Mid	March 2000 (Dot-com burst)	Apr-03	Yes	No	₹2.68 crore	₹2.40 crore
Franklin Bluechip	December 2007 (Sub-prime crisis)	Jan-11	Yes	Yes	₹0.85 crore	₹1.31 crore
Mirae Large Cap	November 2010 (Corruption scandals, policy- paralysis period)	Dec-13	Yes	No	₹2.33 crore	₹1.12 crore
Axis Bluechip	October 2016 (Demonetization, GST, Covid crisis)	Nov-16	No	No	₹0.94 crore	₹0.77 crore

Source: Data collated from NAV data of the MF schemes and analysed by the author

periods. It showcases how the time period of investment and the point at which you start withdrawing your salary–pension could impact your corpus.

A point to note here is that the names of the schemes representing particular scenarios are not relevant. I have analysed all the schemes for all the scenarios, and, with one or two exceptions, nearly all the schemes performed similarly in the given time period. The scheme choice to represent a particular scenario was selected at random.

For example, let's say you had a ₹1 crore corpus with HDFC Balanced Advantage Fund in February 1994, and you started withdrawing 1 per cent from it from March 1994. Then, even without the three-year buffer and without needing to dip into the two-year emergency fund, your corpus would still be worth ₹23.39 crore, and you would have already withdrawn ₹3.49 crore from it.

Similarly, let's say you went with ICICI Prudential Large & Mid Cap Fund and had ₹1 crore in it by March 2000. This was when the dot-com bubble burst, and without a three-year volatility buffer, your corpus would have suffered. If you waited and started withdrawing your 1 per cent salary–pension from April 2003, your corpus would have grown to ₹2.68 crore, and you would have already withdrawn ₹2.40 crore from it.

If your planned salary–pension coincided with the sub-prime crisis in 2007–08, then your corpus would be the worst hit. Even with the three-year wait, you'd need to dip into your emergency funds. But with these protections in place, your corpus would have a good chance of recovery and growth.

Essentially, by adding this waiting period and emergency funding to your diversified portfolio, you are giving your corpus the robustness it needs to sustain your salary–pension. In the best-case scenario, you add significantly to your corpus; in the worst-case scenario, profits catch up and your corpus stays closer to its original value.

Stage 3: Financial Freedom

The final stage of the 1 per cent formula is when you start a systematic withdrawal plan (SWP).

Once you have built your corpus and let it stabilize, it is time to reap your rewards. You can then set up an SWP to withdraw a fixed amount every month. Calculate 1 per cent of your original corpus amount and set that as your monthly SWP. Over time, your original corpus should stabilize to a higher value. You can revisit the 1 per cent calculation every four–five years and set a new, higher SWP amount. The investment professional you engage with can help you decide how to proceed based on the health of your corpus and market conditions.

Remember that in wealth building, everything is gradual. The same applies to using that wealth as well. Don't make big withdrawals from your funds at the same time. You need to nurture them. If you see big withdrawals coming up, plan for them. For example, if you need to pay ₹40 lakh as fees for your child's education, don't take that out at once. Take it out bit by bit over the course of a few years. Similarly, if you have used up the emergency fund, replenish it gradually.

Systematic withdrawal plans help you to maintain a disciplined approach to investing even at the time of withdrawals. It also brings in the advantage of RCA, eliminating the need to time the market. For example, let's say that you had put ₹1 lakh in Axis Bluechip Fund in January 2019 at an NAV of ₹27.09 and, in 2020, you had wanted to withdraw ₹60,000 from it. Here's how it could have looked like:

Lump-Sum Withdrawal					
Month	Cashflows	NAV	No. of Units Redeemed	Fund Units	Fund Value
Jan 2019	1,00,000	27.09		3,699.4	1,00,000
2020					
July	-60,000	29.01	-2,068.3	1,631.1	47,320
Aug	–	29.85	–	1,631.1	48,690
Sept	–	31.10	–	1,631.1	50,729
Oct	–	31.14	–	1,631.1	50,794
Nov	–	32.05	–	1,631.1	52,278
Dec	–	35.75	–	1,631.1	58,313

Systematic Withdrawal Plan					
Month	Cashflows	NAV	No. of Units Redeemed	Fund Units	Fund Value
Jan 2019	1,00,000	27.09		3,699.4	1,00,000
2020					
July	-10,000	29.01	-344.7	3,354.7	97,320
Aug	-10,000	29.85	-335.0	3,019.7	90,138
Sept	-10,000	31.10	-321.5	2,698.1	83,912
Oct	-10,000	31.14	-321.1	2,377.0	74,020
Nov	-10,000	32.05	-312.0	2,065.0	66,183
Dec	-10,000	35.75	-279.7	1,785.3	63,824

In general, an SWP is more beneficial than lump-sum withdrawals as it protects you against market fluctuations by averaging out the NAV. In hindsight, you may feel that you could have timed the market to withdraw a lump-sum at the high point. But, as we discussed before, that is not a good strategy to adopt, especially for an individual investor, so we should always fight that urge to time the markets. Other than being less risky, SWPs are also quite tax-efficient, as each withdrawal is considered to be a combination of capital and income. And so, you pay tax (long-term capital gains[2]) only on the income component at a rate, which is currently just 10%.[3]

BEATING INFLATION WITH THE 1 PER CENT FORMULA

If you look at the returns from EMFs over the last 10 years or since their inception, they have consistently given double digit growth—much more than any of the more tangible or presumably safe assets (Table 9).

Table 9
Growth of EMFs

Sample Diversified EMFs	Age (Yrs)	Returns since Inception (CAGR)	Returns in the Last 10 Yrs (CAGR)
Aditya Birla SL Flexi-cap	24.6	21.00%	15.73%
DSP Equity Opp	22.9	16.83%	15.41%
Franklin Ind Flexi-cap	28.5	17.38%	15.03%
HDFC Flexi-cap	28.3	18.18%	15.23%

---

[2] Provided the investments have completed one year before the withdrawal.
[3] 10 per cent, does not include applicable surcharge or cess.

ICICI Pru Multicap	28.5	14.32%	15.00%
Kotak Equity Opp	18.5	17.61%	15.99%
Mirae Asset Largecap	14.9	14.65%	15.90%
Nippon Ind Multicap	18	16.75%	14.74%
SBI Focused Equity	18.5	18.07%	15.01%
Sundaram Multicap	22.5	14.70%	15.76%

Source: Data collated and calculated from the 2023 factsheet of the mentioned MFs.

While year on year the returns may be inconsistent, on an average, the 1 per cent formula reservoir gets filled by 15–18 per cent yearly returns. When you do start withdrawing from it, you only take out 1 per cent every month, which is around 12 per cent per year coming out from the reservoir. That still leaves an extra 3–5 per cent yearly in the reservoir! With this extra, in the long-term, we can keep increasing our withdrawal amount periodically. This extra is the formula's answer to rising prices!

We saw earlier that the next decade is set to be India's decade. Leading experts on economic growth are confident that the Indian economy is set to be in a phase of vibrancy. The projected figures are looking better than all the previous decades. Expectations from stock markets and EMFs are that the returns will also be as good, if not better than the long-term average. At the same time, inflation in the next decade is projected to be a moderate 4–5 per cent.

So, even in a base case scenario, the figures do add up for the 1 per cent formula to not just provide you your financial freedom but also take care of rising prices in future.

CAN WE PUT OFF THE WORST CASE SCENARIO?

While the numbers may look great, it is important to know that when it comes to our money, we crave for some certainty. So, could we do something more to remove the worry of a worst case scenario playing out? Certainly!

You can make the 1 per cent formula completely future-ready and inflation proof by adding one more protective layer to the formula. To add this additional protection to your future, increase the target corpus amount to 125 times your monthly requirement instead of 100 times as set out earlier.

Let me put this in another way. Let's say after retirement, you don't spend all of your salary–pension as expenses or you still continue to get some side income from passion pursuits. That means you aren't spending all of the 1 per cent you can withdraw monthly. Some of it can stay in the corpus and continue to grow. If this is the case, then even at 100 times, your current income/salary is a future-proof corpus.

But if you are not expecting any kind of income after you quit the rat race, or if you just don't want to worry about your finances or rising prices and are depending on the 1 per cent formula completely, create a corpus worth 125 times of your current income/salary. Just this addition, with everything else remaining the same (three-year volatility buffer and two years emergency fund), will give you a future-proof retirement income.

KEY TAKEAWAYS AND REFLECTIONS

1. The 1 per cent formula has three stages:
    a) Build a corpus worth 100 times your current monthly income

b) Wait for it to stabilize for three years
c) Withdraw 1 per cent from the corpus each month and enjoy your financial freedom
2. Let your corpus stabilize for three years to protect it against market risk. In this time, create an emergency corpus equivalent to two years of expenses.
3. Set up SWPs to help maximize gains from your investments.

CHEW ON THIS

1. What is the salary–pension corpus you need to build, and how will you go about it?
2. Can you replace your term-life and medical insurance policies with EMFs?
3. How old are you now, and by what age would you want to retire? What do you have to do to get there?

7

Making the 1 per cent Formula Work for Your Unique Needs

Sometime around mid-2010, I met Dr Kanawala, an attendee in one of our investor meets. We had done an extensive presentation on the prospects of the Indian economy and made a case for investors to continue to take the benefits by investing in EMF schemes. Throughout the presentation Dr Kanawala kept interrupting to ask questions and, in a one-on-one conversation after that, announced that he was 'completely unconvinced'! I agreed to meet him at his clinic after a couple of days to discuss further.

My meeting with Dr Kanawala at his clinic started with the same words—completely unconvinced. Then he started to elaborate his reasons. 'The proof of the pudding is in the eating—just have a look at my MF portfolio, it has given me negative returns since I started investing 5 years ago!'

I was confused! The fact was that the Sensex had delivered above-average returns of around 22 per cent CAGR in the previous five years, almost all the diversified EMF schemes had delivered better than the Sensex. How could someone have had negative returns?

I then requested to have a look at his portfolio statements, and that is where the mystery unfolded.

Dr Kanawala had invested in every sector and thematic fund possible. From agriculture funds, infrastructure funds and power funds to world gold mining funds—the list was long but did not have a single diversified scheme.

'I listen to experts in the financial news channels for two hours every day and have been investing in the best sectors,' he told me.

A look at his statements made me realize that he had been shifting between funds in new sectors almost every year, most of the time after the stocks prices of companies in the sector had already moved up substantially, as he was basing his decisions on past returns! Then, after entering the new sector, almost every time, he rode the downturns and therefore got the negative returns!

From being a dermatologist, Dr Kanawala had ventured into becoming a fund manager. Based on no relevant qualifications, he was deciding which sector(s) to invest in at any given point of time.

That is when I gave the good doctor a taste of his own medicine and wrote this on a piece of paper:

Diagnosis

- Comatose portfolio due to self-prescribed high-risk over-the-counter EMFs
- Frequent churning

Remedy

- Avoid advice from all financial channels and newspapers
- Invest only in diversified EMFs—once monthly

INVESTING IS NOT A PASTIME

During my long years in the MF industry, I have come across many investors who have approached me to analyse their choices of MF schemes. These interactions have given me some very interesting insights into investor behaviour and how their decisions spoil their experience with the most rewarding asset class.

Indian investors are spoilt for choice—there are thousands of schemes coming from over 40 MF houses. There are many new funds on offer almost every week! Choosing which scheme to invest in can be confusing.

I've seen many people make lesser returns than the markets or, worse still, lesser returns than that delivered by the underlying schemes in their own portfolio. Why does that happen? It's because they don't make the correct choices. Even when they do, they don't stick to a choice once it's made. In an attempt to time the markets, they make frequent exits and re-entries and the very reason to come to an expert fund manager gets diluted.

The Finfluencer Trap

Large cap, mid cap, small cap, cyclicals, value, growth, defensives, dollar-hedge, financials, big-tech, emerging markets, blockchain, bear-market-rally, cautiously optimistic and some other brilliantly coined word-plays are terms used by so called finfluencers in the stock market world.

These finfluencers could be unknown people on TV in the business channels, or the social media influencers talking about trading, or known people like your bank relationship manager.

Whoever they may be, their standard operating procedure is the same—to give you irrelevant, jargonized information about aspects of the stock markets. They are providing you with a delusion of knowledge and a false sense of expertise with the intention to coax you into buying a financial product that you do not need.

There is an entire industry churning out hot-stock-tips that reach WhatsApp accounts of lakhs of investors each morning. It does keep everybody excited about the stock markets but it never makes anybody richer, probably apart from the stock broker himself. Access to some (mostly publicly available) information about the stock makes a lay-investor feel like an expert, a fund manager, and that is the sentiment that gets exploited. Even those who invest in MFs expect 'new ideas' and are gladly provided with a whole gambit of new fund offers (NFOs), different sector or thematic funds or new exotic products with complicated structures. It basically runs like the fashion industry with in-fashion schemes and a new collection coming out every season.

What I want you to understand is that stock-market investment expertise comes to professionals from years of experience. They make it their full-time job as opposed to someone for whom it is just a hobby or a part-time effort. Most successful fund managers rely on the collective efforts of a large team of professionals who research sectors and track individual companies for years to make informed decisions on buying or selling stocks from the multitude of choices.

If you want to take investing up as a hobby, that's your call. But then, be very clear that it is a hobby and not investing for your future. Investing is an area of expertise where operating from limited information is dangerous.

Once you are able to distinguish between investing and taking up a hobby, you can easily make a distinction between the finfluencers and the real experts. One set of people is giving us excitement and the other is playing an important role in securing our financial future. Interacting with one set can give us a lot of pleasure and excitement over a pastime, but after identifying the other set, we can sit back, relax and enjoy boring financial freedom!

Yes, boring—at least for people who rather look forward to that day-trading tip along with their morning cuppa. But here is some advice from some of the best wealth creators I know:

> Creating wealth should be the most boring task for investors once they have identified the experts. All the excitement and hustle-bustle should be at the fund manager's desk.
>
> Dabbling in stocks without the know-how and expertise is gambling. It is not investing—be ready to lose some money!

But then if you can't invest on the latest market tip or 'advice' from finfluencers, what can you do?

MEET THE FRIENDLY NEIGHBOURHOOD INVESTMENT PROFESSIONAL

Are you wondering why we are talking about investment professionals?

Aren't they all out to sell you schemes and insurance plans that you don't need?

Why should you pay them to manage your money when this book has already given you everything you need to know?

Well, think of it this way.

An investment professional is like your fitness instructor. It's not that you don't know how to exercise or eat well; it's the discipline that takes work. Your fitness instructor is there to tell you when you are lagging behind and what you can do to fix it. They keep track of new developments in the fitness space and keep you updated so you can make informed choices. And that's what an investment professional does with your money.

Investment professionals know their stuff. To get a licence to operate as an investment professional, they need to pass a test every three years. They are tested on their knowledge of the latest rules and regulations and taxation laws governing the industry. For example, until a few years ago, dividends received through dividend plans (later named Income Distribution cum Capital Withdrawal [IDCW] plans) in MF schemes were tax-free; now, they are taxable and get added to your other income. In this case, opting for growth plans makes more sense—something an investment professional can advise you on. Such changes in rules, regulations and tax laws keep happening, and investment professionals are obligated to be up to date on these things.

An investment professional is your guide on your journey to financial freedom. They help you make the right decisions and keep you on track when you might make panic-driven or emotional choices. Their biggest contribution is helping you stay focussed on disciplined investing.

Most of us lead busy lives. There is so much that demands our time and attention—deliverables at work, responsibilities at home and the daily routines of life. Where is the time to think about and plan for financial freedom? Who can prioritize investing when there is just so much going on in life!

Your boss wanted that presentation yesterday.

Your kids' school called a parent–teacher meeting.

Your parents are grousing that you don't have time for them.

Your friends want you at every get-together.

Your gym instructor gives you a stink-eye if you miss even one day.

You have a dentist appointment to go to.

How can you even think about where your money is going? At best, you can take out maybe an hour a month.

But is that enough? Not really, and so you keep delaying investment decisions. Finance isn't your first priority.

You aren't alone in delaying investment decisions because you never found time for it. Or if you did invest, at best, it was haphazard, and you never really gave it a second look.

Most of the clients who come to me don't lack financial intelligence; they lack financial diligence. Their finances are a mess! They invest randomly, don't pay attention to detail and, in some cases, they do not even have nominees in their MF or bank accounts! And that's the case with most people. As an investment professional, my role is to help my clients put all this in order and put their financial health first. After all, it's my job, and, hence, my first priority.

I had a couple who came to me after unsuccessfully trying to start investing for their retirement. The man, Alok, was at a good position in the investment banking sector and gave mergers and acquisitions advice to medium to large corporates with a specialization in the FMCG sector. He knew the ins and outs of the working of the eight to 10 companies that he had closely worked with in his career and had a reasonably good knowledge about how the share markets worked in the sector. He always considered personal finance as an extension of what he did with the corporates and while he thought he could manage a do-it-yourself, he never had the time because he was so busy with managing the finances for his clients. Whatever little 'portfolio' construction he could do had a skew towards the FMCG sector.

So, we sat down together and created a financial plan, and then, he passed the baton to me to keep the plan on track. It's been a lasting relationship, and I have had the privilege of growing their portfolio many times over. And the best part of working with them is that they know the industry and are able to appreciate my choices and suggestions better.

So even if you know the market or the ins and outs of investing, you may still need an advisor. In fact, you need an advisor more, if you think you know everything about the market! Leo Buscaglia, an American author, said, 'Those who think they know it all have no way of finding out they don't.' An investment advisor is also your protection against your blind spots. They, as a neutral third party, can point out when your decisions deviate from facts and become emotional instead.

Viraat, an old friend of mine, had called me one day to seek some advice on 'a few insurance policies' that he had. I was surprised to look at the list. Here was a person who was a successful second-generation entrepreneur owning an exports-oriented business empire of a few hundred crore turnover. He had around 15 traditional life-insurance policies that covered him for a total of ₹55 lakh and a couple of medical insurance policies covering just about ₹4-5 lakh in medical expenses. There was an investment part to the life insurance policies as well that, on an average, gave a pitiful 4.5 per cent annualized return, that too only if he kept paying the premiums for another 15 years.

I couldn't bear it! I told him, 'So, if you pass away someday, your family will get an additional ₹55 lakh apart from the 500 crore worth shareholding in your business? Ridiculous! And, weren't you bragging to me the other day that your business gives you a return on equity of a double-digit percentage? Absolutely outrageous!'

I may have exaggerated a little about his net worth, but I wanted to make a point or two!

Then he confided in me that the 15 policies were all sold to him by relatives and friends from time to time and he had to oblige, given the relationships.

The truth is that most people who are sold insurance products don't need it. And those who really do need it don't get the right product choice (term-insurance) on offer!

Anyway, after pulling Viraat's leg for quite some time that day, I then advised him to surrender all the policies and, instead, focus his personal investment efforts towards diversifying into other sectors of the economy. We discussed how the world economy is expected to slow down in the coming decade, so he needed to diversify and place more bets on domestic businesses. He may not be able to do that through his business, but certainly by investing all his surplus cash in diversified EMFs.

As I mentioned before, investment professionals also shine a light on your blind spots and keep your portfolio updated. They keep track of not just the investment opportunities but regulatory changes, changes in fund management teams, shift in the investment strategy, need for insurance and so on, and make timely recommendations. Most of these investment professionals also liaise with financial institutions, CAs and lawyers and can get you personalized advice on succession planning, overall tax planning, etc.—synergizing your investments with all other areas of financial planning. And you can rest easy in the knowledge that your money is in capable hands. Of course, that doesn't mean you get to ignore your investments. You still need to keep an eye on them, but you can avoid focussing on the minute details that go into it.

Another reason why you really need to look for an investment professional early on is that they can streamline your financial planning. Let's be honest, how many of us are thinking of retirement in our late 20s or early 30s? It sounds like something really far into the future, isn't it? Similarly, when we are young, we don't really think about contingency planning. What if something was to go wrong?

An investment professional brings in a lot of insights from dealings with other clients to make a comprehensive plan keeping in mind multiple scenarios where you might need your money to work for you. And they keep you on track. For example, my youngest clients are my sister and brother-in-law, both in their late 20s. My senior-most clients are the parents of a friend, retired and in their 70s. And two of my clients have children who are finishing college, ready to start their careers. Their life stories, goals and situations are completely different, and this gives me a rich perspective that I can share with my other clients.

It is well and good to know that markets are volatile, but it is not easy to stay put when you see your wealth depleted in a matter of days. Then, all the math goes out of the window, and you are left to operate from fear of losing your life's work. And the markets may not recover immediately. It may take them some time—even a few years—to recover. That is, again, where the investment professional acts as your anchor. They are able to give you the reassurance that things will be well again. They will keep track of the big picture of your overall personal finances and can be your guide or best friend in all your financial decision-making, especially in times when emotions run high.

I was managing the finances of an elderly couple. When the Covid-19 crisis hit and markets saw a steep drop, they lost 30 per cent of their wealth in the crash. Every day I was getting frantic calls from them, and all they wanted to do was to salvage what was there and take out all the money from equity funds. That would have been a disaster for them as they would not have recovered what they lost, and they didn't have an income source or the time to build a fresh corpus. It took all my persuasion skills to get them to stay invested and not exit. It was almost like counselling them because they were so worried. It is natural. If, in your late 60s, you suddenly lose 30 per cent of your wealth, you would worry too. So, we had many conversations and lengthy discussions, and they agreed to stay invested in their current portfolio. In a matter of months, the market bounced back and they not only recovered what they lost but ended up adding to their wealth. If they did not have an investment advisor, they might have been badly burnt from this experience.

Investment professionals help keep tabs on your salary–pension corpus even after it is built. For example, to manage volatility after retirement, they could advise you to move some percentage of your corpus to a balanced advantage fund of the same fund house. This might come at the cost of slightly lower returns but helps you align better with your changing risk-taking abilities.

Getting an investment advisor on board is well worth

their fee. The key is in getting the right advisor—someone who has integrity and whom you can trust. A good way to build this trust is by being aware and involved in the process. When your advisor recommends a fund to you, think back on the learning from this book and see if that is a good recommendation. Some unscrupulous advisors might recommend funds where they earn a higher commission but which is not really a good investment choice. Others try to gain your trust at first and then recommend bundling good funds with bad, extremely expensive insurance products that, eventually, only take care of their financial interests, not yours. These unsavoury elements give the whole community a bad name. So, take your time in evaluating your investment professionals, looking over their suggestions and building trust over time.

Role of the Investment Professional in Your Journey to Financial Freedom

Building wealth through the 1 per cent formula is certainly easier than random investments. However, working with an investment professional can make this journey even more profitable and rewarding by giving it tailored attention. They can guide you on your wealth-building journey with consideration to your specific needs and distinct financial goals.

Here are some ways in which an investment professional can add value to your pursuit of early retirement:

1. Setting the right goals for your unique needs and circumstances: They will look at your existing resources, understand your salary–pension objectives and help you set achievable goals at every stage of the process.

2. Making the right investment decisions and creating a tailor-made investment plan: They can help you rejig your assets in a way that accelerates your path to the salary–pension corpus. They can also weigh in on the funds you select, helping you choose better options based on your risk profile and the time period left till retirement. All the investment decisions are customized to your needs.
3. Actively managing the corpus: They can make recommendations to switch your corpus to other funds based on prevalent market conditions or personal circumstances. For example, looking at your risk profile, your investment professional may recommend shifting a percentage (even up to 50 per cent) of your corpus during the cushion period into balanced advantage funds that offer slightly reduced volatility at the cost of slightly reduced returns. Or, when there's a stronger case to do so, they may recommend shifting a certain percentage of your corpus in passive funds or any new category as the case may be.
4. Tracking fund managers and fund houses: The investment professional keeps an eye on the industry. In case the fund manager you picked leaves the fund you are invested in and joins another company; the investment professional can advise you on whether you should remain invested or exit. They can also alert you to any unethical practices and help you steer clear of them.
5. Planning withdrawals in a way that doesn't imbalance your corpus: An investment professional can help

you plan for large withdrawals in a systematic way. As your salary pension corpus grows, they can also help you decide when and by how much to increase the withdrawals to adjust for inflation while making sure the corpus retains its stability. They can help you decide when it makes more sense to dip into the emergency corpus, given the market conditions and the state of your salary pension corpus. What's more, they can help you replenish the emergency corpus gradually so that it is available the next time you need it.
6. Bringing in an eye for detail and a penchant for due process: An investment professional can point out little things that make a big difference—for example, adding a second holder and putting a nomination in the application forms across all your investments.

While an investment advisor in your corner is recommended, many people may still choose to manage their portfolios by themselves, and that is fine. As long as they are careful to not fall in the same trap that Dr Kanawala did. If you prefer to manage your own investments, the main question is: how do you decide what goes in your portfolio?

Here is what might be going on in your mind: 'EMFs can lead me to my financial nirvana, but which one(s)? There are thousands of schemes to choose from! There are more than 40 MF houses! How do I evaluate which fund managers or fund management teams are good?'

The answer lies in one word—diversification.

WHEN IT COMES TO INVESTING IN EQUITY MUTUAL FUNDS, THE MANTRA IS DIVERSIFICATION

You see, as I mentioned earlier, the stock markets list around 5,000 companies from 30 different sectors, and each sector may have a unique cycle of earnings and growth. For example, there are the 'defensive' sectors constituted by companies catering to essential goods and services, like consumer staples and utilities, where growth follows a long and steady trend, and the share prices are somewhat immune to overall market volatility. On the other hand, there are sectors like automobile manufacturers, hospitality companies, etc., where the segment itself is termed as 'Cyclicals' as their performance follows the trends in the overall economy with all its fluctuations. Then there are sectors that cater to exports, where there is a dependency on the economic trends of other countries.

Even market cap-based company groups (large, mid and small) can experience cycles due to the group behaviour of market participants. So, it is best to diversify your funds across sectors and market caps.

In addition to this, there can be some irrational turns and cycles in the markets caused by euphoric buying/selling activity among investor groups or sharp reactions to major domestic and global events.

Even today, everybody remembers the sharp rise and fall in our markets in the early 1990s caused by the Harshad Mehta scandal. One market cycle was the tech boom-and-crash in the period from early 1999 to early 2000. And who can forget the steep fall in markets across the globe after the 9/11 terrorist attack in the US. Another cycle began in our markets with a mounting interest in the real estate, power utilities and NBFC sectors and ended with the big global crash following the US sub-prime crisis in 2007–08. Currently, too, the world is witnessing what seems like the end of yet another cycle. It began with the Covid-19 crisis when central banks gave support to their industries by increasing liquidity, which sustained growth but also resulted in multi-decadal-high inflation rates. Now we see liquidity tightening measures being taken by the same central banks, thereby ending a cycle of liquidity led growth. I know that doesn't sound like a good thing, but it is normal behaviour. In the long run, even with crashes, markets show an upward trend in line with the growth of the economy.

To mitigate the impact of these cycles—of the markets and the sectors—you need to diversify your portfolio.

That essentially means choosing a competent fund manager with experience in three to four market cycles and giving them the freedom to choose which stocks to invest in. Based on how the markets and sectors move, fund managers can change investment strategies to continue delivering value to the investors. Usually, a fund with 40–60 stocks of big and small companies across five-to-seven unrelated sectors reduces risks considerably. Additionally, this helps the fund manager to choose from the best performing companies in all sectors. So, reduce risk and choose from the best—a winning strategy!

A point to note here is that different schemes may have different sector weightages for a portfolio strategy, you need to be patient to allow the scheme to let the sector cycles play out. Short-term performance comparisons can trigger unwarranted churning and lead to a poor experience with equities (as an asset class).

In addition, it is a good idea to diversify your portfolio

from a management perspective. So, opt for one or two schemes, each from three to five different fund houses. Going with large fund houses is always a better option since they can put together a strong team with the necessary tools required to gather the needed intelligence. According to SEBI regulations, a large fund also charges you less, while the smaller funds are more expensive to invest in. So, it makes sense to go with the larger ones.

Holding six to 10 different schemes across three to five fund houses is quite sufficient to get a good, diversified portfolio!

FUND MANAGERS MATTER!

Fund managers are the people who are effectively deciding where your money goes. Before deciding to invest in an EMF scheme, it's a good idea to vet the credentials of the fund manager.

There are thousands of funds and hundreds of fund managers in India, but only a few have the experience and the analytical capability to make sound investing decisions.

Previously, I have talked about my team and how meticulous it was in evaluating a company's ability to make profits—that was its benchmark. A good fund manager will invest in a strong company and not on the basis of market sentiment. They will have the pulse of the industry and the economy as a whole, not just the pulse of the market. Having experienced three to four market cycles, they know how to steer the fund through ups and downs. And they have the mettle to make decisions—even unpopular ones—on the basis of this extensive analysis.

I have spoken about my mentor Prashant Jain previously, and I can unapologetically say that he is one of the finest, most balanced fund managers in the world today. I recall the late 1990s, when the dot-com bubble burst. Many star fund managers from that time sank into oblivion because they couldn't stand the test of that one cycle. They were heavily invested in the tech sector because that was the flavour of the season. They were just not able to survive the dot-com crash.

Prashant, on the other hand, always had the pulse of the markets. I clearly remember, he wrote in a factsheet in December 1999 that he has completely exited from the technology sector. This was a time when the prices of technology company shares were doubling every month. But he stuck his neck out and exited. And just two months after that, the bubble burst. While few of the fund managers lost up to 80 per cent of the fund value, he was able to preserve most of it. The regulator has since made stricter rules to limit single sector exposure and single company exposure.

Similarly, many fund managers who had overinvested in the sectors of real-estate, infrastructure and power utilities in 2007–08 depleted the fund value substantially in the sub-prime crisis. There was an extremely popular IPO at time—that company is now close to bankruptcy. Market cycles really test the mettle of fund managers and their ability to come out of these crashes unscathed. This is why it's really important to research your fund manager and choose wisely.

The profiles of fund managing teams are available on the fund website. Take some time to go through them and check their experience.

How have they performed in the past?

Have they experienced at least three to four market cycles?

Do they have enough resources to do an in-depth analysis?

What are some of the decisions they have taken in the face of a crisis?

When choosing a scheme and a fund manager, always look at their long-term performance track record. Short-term performance can be misleading and heavily influenced by the market and sector cycles.

Experienced fund managers attract more investors, giving them larger funds to manage, and, as I mentioned earlier, that reduces the charges they levy—a win-win for the investor!

While a competent fund manager will do their utmost to create value for their schemes, as an individual investor, you need to diversify your portfolio across schemes and EMF categories. The categories of EMFs have been defined by the regulator and determine where that fund can invest. Some of these categories clash with our criterion of diversification. This is why choosing the right fund is extremely important. Here's how you should spread your investments across fund categories:

Category of Funds	Flexibility to Diversify across Sectors	Flexibility to Diversify across Company Size	Suggested Allocation (%)
Flexi-cap Fund*	Complete flexibility	Complete flexibility	60–100
Multi-cap Fund Large and Mid-cap Fund Large-cap	Complete flexibility	Defined limits	20–40
Focussed Fund	Limit on no. of stocks	Complete flexibility	0–20

Mid-cap Fund Small-cap Fund	Complete flexibility	Defined limits	0
Dividend Yield Fund Value Fund Contra Fund	Flexible but situational	Flexible but situational	0
Sector/Thematic Fund	Restricted	Limited within the sector(s)	0
*Add Equity Linked Savings Schemes (ELSS) Fund here, exclusively for availing Section 80C Tax benefit (three-year lock-in)			

A NEW INVESTOR'S GUIDE TO EQUITY MUTUAL FUNDS

If you are a new investor, understanding the various types of EMFs can get confusing. So here is a quick guide for your ready reference.

Equity MFs are mainly categorized based on four criteria:

1. Investment strategy
2. Market capitalization of invested companies
3. Tax treatment
4. Investment style

Here are the key fund types in each of these categories:

Investment strategy	Market capitalization
• Sectoral • Thematic • Focussed • Contra • Value	• Large-Cap • Mid-Cap • Small-Cap • Multi-Cap • Large and Mid-Cap • Flexi-Cap
Tax treatment	Investment style
• ELSS • Non-Tax Saving	• Active • Passive

Let's understand each of these fund types to understand what they offer, and which ones are best suited for the 1 per cent formula.

1. **Sectoral funds:** These are equity funds that only invest in a particular sector, like banking, IT, pharmaceutical, etc. If you choose to invest in this type of fund, you are restricting your investments to a particular sector. During a down-cycle of this sector, the fund manager cannot shift to companies from sectors moving up-cycle. I would recommend you steer clear of these funds.

2. **Thematic funds:** These are funds that choose stocks to invest in based on a certain theme, such as rural consumption, exports and services, ESG and so on. Thematic funds can pick companies across sectors that are aligned to the central theme of the fund. These are more diversified than sectoral funds but have similar limitations. Here again, the fund manager is limited by the theme and cannot pick high-performing stocks if they do not align with it. Steer clear of this category as well.

3. **Focussed funds:** Focussed funds invest in only a limited number of stocks—a maximum of 30. The advantage of these types of funds is that they offer diversification across sectors and company sizes. Also, given that the number of stocks is limited, fund managers spend more time and effort in selecting these stocks. A higher concentration of stocks makes these a high-risk, high-return portfolio.
4. **Contra funds:** These funds follow a contrarian strategy of investing. They invest in stocks that are currently out-of-favour in the markets. Typically, underperformers are picked at low price points with a view that they will perform in the long run.
5. **Value funds:** These funds follow a value investing strategy. They invest in undervalued stocks with better performance prospects in future as value unlocks.
6. **Large-cap funds:** These funds invest 80–100 per cent of their total assets in shares of large-cap companies—the current top 100 by market cap as defined by the market regulator. These are considered more stable than the mid-cap or small-cap oriented funds and could form a decent chunk of your investment portfolio.
7. **Mid-cap funds:** These funds invest around 65 per cent of their total assets in mid-cap companies (currently those ranking 101–250 by market cap as defined by the regulator). A small percentage of your portfolio may be considered for this category.
8. **Small-cap funds:** These funds invest around 65 per cent of their total assets in small-cap companies (beyond the 250 rank by market cap) and could be highly volatile. Again, a very small percentage may be considered for the portfolio.
9. **Large and mid-cap funds:** These funds invest equally in

large and mid-cap companies and offer lower volatility with better returns. You may consider investing in these if they are managed by a good fund manager.
10. **Multi-cap funds:** These funds allocate 25 per cent of their assets each to small-, mid-, and large-cap stocks. The fund manager has the flexibility to rebalance the portfolio depending on the market conditions, company performance and investment objective of the scheme. This is a good investment option if driven by an experienced fund manager.
11. **Flexi-cap funds:** This is the best choice of funds. Flexi-cap funds have the leeway to dynamically invest in all kinds of stocks without restrictions on the market cap. This allows the fund managers to make investment choices that will deliver the best outcomes for the fund. If you want to make life simple for yourself and narrow down your choice of funds from only one category, Flexi-cap is that category!
12. **Equity linked savings scheme:** These funds offer tax benefits of up to ₹1.5 lakh under Section 80C of the Income Tax Act. The drawback is the three-year lock-in period. Invest in these funds if you need the tax write-off.
13. **Passive funds:** These funds track a market index or segment to choose the stocks for investment without the active involvement of the fund manager. This is a very popular category in the more developed markets where actively managed funds rarely beat the indices. We can avoid this category for a few more years in favour of schemes managed by some of our finely skilled fund managers.

KEY TAKEAWAYS AND REFLECTIONS

1. Diversify your portfolio, both in terms of types of funds and fund houses.
2. Invest in flexi-cap or multi-cap funds with an active fund manager. Stay away from sectoral and thematic funds. Invest in ELSS only to the extent of your need to save taxes.
3. Put some effort into finding the right fund and fund manager. Check their experience and the team's track record in terms of performance.
4. Get an investment professional on board to help you navigate this journey with ease.

CHEW ON THIS

1. Which are some of the top funds and fund managers in the country?
2. Who can act as your investment advisor, and how will you evaluate their credibility?

8

Success Stories of the 1 per cent Formula

Over the course of my career, I have had the chance to discuss personal finance with people from different walks of life with different income levels, levels of aspirations, savings patterns and understanding of money. Here are some of the stories where we've effectively met the goals and aspirations of people from different walks of life.[1]

Financial Security

---

[1] The names and some details have been modified in the stories for confidentiality.

STARTING AFRESH, NO SAVINGS: THE ARMY MAN

Objective: To fund his children's education abroad

Eight years ago, sometime in mid-2015, Lt. Col. Sarvadarshi Pant (or 'Sporty', as we know him), one among the many batch mates from my school who had joined the armed forces, called me. He had decided to 'hang his boots' and do something else.

Like any efficient, large organization, the hierarchy of the Indian Army becomes quite narrow at the top. Among the large number of mid-level officers, only a few get the much-sought-after promotion. From the ones that miss out, a few start musing about a career outside, in the civilian world. While officers may decide to quit the army earlier, it is only after 20 years of service that they can choose to take premature retirement with eligibility to pension benefits. One of the most wonderful HR practices that the armed forces now employ is that they make these officers job-ready for the outside world before they are let go. On offer are management courses from any premier institute in the country. Sporty went on to do an army-sponsored six-month business management course from Indian Institute of Management (IIM) Ahmedabad.

Ex-army personnel are quite sought after by the corporate world for their spirited leadership skills and the values that they bring to the table—the values of discipline, integrity and hard work. But at the time Sporty had quit the Indian Army, the job scene was not very encouraging. It took him more than a year to find a suitable job with a respectable organization. The pay was a little lower than what he used to draw from the army, but he was confident that there was scope for growth in the years to come. He was 45 and was looking at a full 15 years of corporate life ahead of him.

Seven years ago, when Sporty had just got his job, he called me again. This time, it was for a very different reason—he wanted to discuss his finances: an Achilles heel for most faujis!'

Sporty's son Angad had received his acceptance letter for the undergraduate course in computer science from one of the best universities in Australia. This was a dream come true for Angad but a cause of worry for his father.

How can we afford this? he thought.

It was only in 2006—mid-way through his tenure—that pay scales had risen in the armed forces with the Sixth Pay Commission coming into effect. Before that, they could not save a lot. Sporty, however, did manage to save up decently for the last 10 years, but he used them to build a house worth ₹55 lakh in an army welfare society in Noida.

The retirement corpus, including the PF that he received from the army, was close to ₹1 crore, along with a pension of ₹50,000 a month.

Last year, with no other source of income, he had to dip into his retirement corpus for Angad's school fees and household expenses and withdraw ₹20 lakh. The corpus, even after bank FD interest, was now reduced to ₹82 lakh. When he did get a job, since his workplace was in Gurgaon, to travel daily from Noida, he had picked up a car on an EMI of ₹17,000. Now, with a ₹2 lakh monthly take-home salary from his new job, could he afford to give his child a foreign education?

We did a quick budgeting exercise:

Cost for the course including travel, etc. = ₹15 lakh per annum
Living expenses for Sporty and his wife = ₹15 lakh per annum
Car EMIs = ₹2 lakh per annum

Total cost: ₹32 lakh per annum
Salary and pension = ₹30 lakh per annum

This was a deficit of ₹2 lakh per year.

We had to now plan the investment in a way that met this deficit while also allowing for future growth.

As a first step, from the ₹82 lakh available, we set aside ₹8 lakh to meet the deficit for four years. This stayed put in a bank FD.

We used the remaining ₹74 lakh to create the retirement corpus in Mirae Large Cap Fund (₹25 lakh); HDFC Flexi-cap Fund (₹25 lakh); and FI Flexi-cap Fund (₹24 lakh). This happened in 2016.

Angad graduated from college in 2020, got a job offer on-campus and started taking care of all his expenses independently. Sporty then started adding ₹1.5 lakh monthly to his EMF portfolio, which stands at a corpus size of ₹2.52 crore at the end of March 2023.

He has understood the 1 per cent formula and is now planning to retire in the next four to five years (including the volatility buffer period) with a corpus of ₹4 crore or a ₹4 lakh monthly salary–pension on top of his army pension.

Life is good!

LOOKING FOR A BETTER LIFE: THE PARENTS

Objective: Daughter's financial independence

I like to believe that all parents want the best for their children. They want their children to not go through the hardships that they went through in their childhood. They want to give them a stronger foundation to build a better life—a better education, occupation, lifestyle and, above all, a better social and financial standing.

Renuka was born and brought up in Raebareli, Uttar Pradesh. Having a conservative upbringing in a small town meant having to deal with strong patriarchal mindset and traditions throughout her childhood. From the choice of education stream to deciding whom to marry, it was her father who made the decisions for her.

Renuka was married into a business family in Delhi, where her daughter Nishka was born. She was determined to bring Nishka up to be a strongly independent person. Renuka's husband Rahul and I went to college together and we met on and off during my Delhi stint.

In 2015, Nishka turned 21, completed her undergraduate degree and started pursuing her master's from the National Institute of Design, Ahmedabad. She was an excellent student and really good at her subject. She had already received offers of some paid internships to create web content for a few start-ups. Her career seemed set!

I met her during one of our social meet-ups and the conversation turned to her future prospects. As a parent, Renuka always wanted more financial security for her only child. They had saved ₹11 lakh in a bank FD and she had also convinced Rahul to save ₹15,000 monthly from his business income to build on Nishka's financial security needs.

As they were telling me this, I could not help but tell them about the fallacy of 'safe' investment assets. And the conversation turned to the 1 per cent formula. Both Renuka and Rahul were convinced of the viability of the formula and asked me to take up investing for Nishka.

As the first step, I converted the ₹11 lakh into EMFs and

started SIPs worth ₹15,000 in the same schemes:

- ₹7 lakh in HDFC Flexi-cap Fund with a ₹9,000 monthly SIP
- ₹4 lakh in FI Focussed Equity Fund with a ₹6,000 monthly SIP

In the eight years since then, Nishka's wealth has grown to ₹51 lakh. Nishka is now 29 and getting married to her college friend. Renuka is happy that she has built a decent safety net for her daughter. As per the 1 per cent formula, in another three years, Nishka could start taking out a monthly income of ₹51,000 from her corpus. Even if she doesn't need the monthly income from this source, the corpus will grow to approximately double every five years, and that, in turn, can be converted into a bigger monthly income at any stage later.

HIGH INCOME, LUXURIOUS LIFESTYLE: THE MERCHANT NAVY MARINER

Objective: Retire early from a demanding job while making sure to have the funds required to continue living a luxurious life

The life of a merchant navy mariner is tough—physically and emotionally, but the pay is good. Usually, a mariner spends a major portion of the year on ship—months at a stretch. That's not everyone's cup of tea. Besides the physical endurance required for the job, being away from home for months not only means having to miss your spouse's birthdays or your friends' weddings but also not being close to a loved one in times of need. On the bright side, the one big compensating factor in this career is the decent pay and the lifestyle that comes along with it.

A few years ago, when I was travelling to Dehradun on a leisure trip, a common friend referred Capt. Ranjit Ahluwalia to me for some investment advice. The 38-year-old had been a seafarer for 14 years and had been quite successful in his career. He had become the youngest marine superintendent of one of the units of the South American oil company that he worked for.

I met Ranjit at his apartment in a posh locality in Dehradun. He introduced me to his homemaker wife, their two children and his old parents. At that time, he was on a 45-days-on and 45-days-off work cycle. On top of that, it took around 40 hours of travel time one way from his workplace in Brazil to be home in Dehradun. This schedule and distance made it impossible for him to be around in cases of emergency. It had happened before when his father had suffered a heart attack a year ago.

When we sat down to discuss investments, Ranjit started by confiding in me about how the rigorous work schedule and all the travel were starting to take a toll on his health and that he wished to move into a more comfortable job closer home in the next five-to-seven years, which would mean much lesser pay. The concern of meeting the costs of sending both of his children to college abroad and settling them down always made him defer any plans of quitting the rigorous life of a mariner.

Ranjit also loved luxury cars and changed his vehicle every three to four years. His dream was to buy a Porsche in the next couple of years. He also wanted to buy an independent bungalow that would cost him around ₹7.5 crore. His two kids would be ready for college in the next three to four years, and for the eight years after that, he would have to budget around ₹40 lakh per year for the education of his children in the US.

At the time we spoke, Ranjit was earning a monthly take-home salary of ₹9–10 lakh. With household expenses of around ₹3 lakh per month, he had the potential to save ₹6–7 lakh per month. The challenge, then, was not the lack of funds, but the way they were managed.

After analysing his existing investments, I realized that there was not much thought behind where he was investing. His money was not working for him. The investments were random, and interestingly, in line with the year's fashionable thing to do! Merchant navy mariners have a close-knit group, and Ranjit was doing what the rest of his colleagues did.

Here's what his investment pattern revealed:

- Spending before investing: Ranjit was doing the exact opposite of one of the 10 commandments of wealth building. His peer group encouraged spending on luxury cars and goods and, in his own words, 'When I see money in the bank, there is an urge to spend.' That didn't leave much for saving.
- Tendency to prefer illiquid investments that are prone to losses: Ranjit had invested a lot in real estate, some of which exhibited negative returns.
- Choosing 'safe' investment options: Most of his liquid investments (almost 70 per cent) were in bank non-resident Indian (NRI) FDs, and the rest in debt and tax-saving MFs. Just about 12 per cent of his liquid portfolio was in EMFs. Together, these investments were giving him an average return of 9 per cent per annum.

When I showed him an excel sheet of his future earnings and expenses, he realized that it's high time he saved before he spent. He decided to shelve the plans for the bungalow and postpone the Porsche for a few more years.

Given his income, aspirations and existing investments, we knew what we had to do.

The mission: Convert the seven-digit salary to a seven-digit return-from-investments using the 1 per cent formula—in seven years.

Our target was to build a corpus of ₹8 crore in seven years that converts to ₹8 lakh a month thereon, as per the 1 per cent formula. Here is how we went about it.

Ranjit began investing all of his savings in EMFs through a monthly SIP of ₹6 lakh. He also converted his existing debt funds to equity funds. He decided to sell off some of the real estate and cut the losses so the proceeds could be put to more productive use in EMFs. He decided to leave the bank FDs in place to take care of his daughter's college expenses for the first two-and-a-half years.

At the end of this exercise, we had the following funds available for the investment plan.

- Lump-sum investment of ₹90 lakh—₹40 lakh from MFs and ₹50 lakh from the sale of real estate
- Monthly SIP of ₹6 lakh

Using the calculator I had shared earlier, you can see how this amount can grow to way over the target ₹8 crore in the given seven-year timeframe.

Ranjit planned to save somewhat less from year six onwards to fund the remainder of his daughter's education, but the corpus itself would be substantial enough to grow on its own, and the 1 per cent withdrawal would help pay for his son's education. And it even leaves room to build the 'Porsche fund'!

Target met!

SINGLE INCOME, COMFORTABLE LIFESTYLE: THE SINGLE MOM

Objective: Achieve financial security for her child so she can stop feeling anxious about earning money and can instead work for her passion.

Mira and her husband Gaurav were a young couple in their early 30s who believed in living life to their fullest. They had a large circle of friends, and, together, they loved to go out and party, buy luxury goods and travel. They both came from lower-middle-income families and their parents had invested all their earnings in getting Mira and Gaurav an education so they could stand on their own feet. The parents' effort had paid off, and both of them were earning well and sending money home. In living well and supporting their households, they did not think much about saving.

They both had an entrepreneurial spirit. Mira always wanted to open a restaurant, and Gaurav was passionate about real estate. After spending seven to eight years working for large multinational companies, they quit their jobs to start out as full-time entrepreneurs. They invested their savings of ₹40 lakh into these two ventures. At the same time, at the age of 32, they also decided to start a family.

And then, the unthinkable happened: Gaurav passed away. Mira was devastated. She was a single mom with no savings and no job. She was too grief-stricken to be able to continue with the restaurant or the real-estate project. So, she closed them both down, losing all the money they had invested in it.

Mira and Gaurav had been talking about financial planning for a while but never got around to it. The only thing they had managed to do was to get a term-life insurance policy of ₹1 crore for each of them. Mira knew that she didn't want to touch this money. She wanted to save it for their child to ensure that his future is secure. But even thinking about money hurt at that time. So, she let the insurance money sit in her bank account for a whole year, where it earned a pittance in interest.

When she was able to think with a bit more clarity, she called me. We knew each other through a common friend. She explained her situation to me and said she wants to invest this money in MFs. Mira was very clear that this money was for her child, and she would rather add to it when she got back on her feet.

So, we invested the money in EMFs, and she kept adding around ₹6 lakh to this every year. In four years, despite the Covid-19 slump, her corpus had grown to ₹2 crore. She believed in the long-term growth story of MFs, and even when she lost ₹30 lakh in the pandemic-led market slump, she heeded my advice and did not withdraw her money. Within a few months, she had recovered that money and added another ₹20 lakh to it as the market shot up again.

In the grim reality of Covid-19, Mira was certain that she didn't want a financially uncertain future for her child. So, she upped her term-life insurance cover to ₹2 crore. That way, in case something happened to her, her child would be left with a corpus of ₹4 crore, enough to take care of all his needs till he attained majority and started earning for himself.

If she continued her present investments for the next five years, her ₹2 crore corpus would grow to ₹4 crore, and she could then opt to stop the term-life insurance. Mira was clear that she did not want to withdraw from this. And even if she stopped adding any more money to this corpus, then, in the next 15 years, when her son would be just out of college, he would have a whopping ₹22 crore at his disposal. So, in the next five years, Mira would have attained freedom from the financial stress and anxiety over her son's future.

But she didn't stop at that. Mira knew that life was fickle. She had been a victim of it. She didn't want her financials to be in a mess in case something happened to her. So, in her late 30s, she made a will that laid down specific instructions to start following the 1 per cent formula for withdrawals to take care of all expenses for her child in the event of her death. Today, her financial assets are neatly tied up and accounted for and are growing even as you read this. By being prudent about money, investing in the right instruments and separating facts from feelings, Mira now lives a stress-free life. After all, whatever happens, she has ensured a good life for her child!

LIVING WELL ON THEIR OWN TERMS: THE NRI COUPLE

Objective: Aim for a comfortable lifestyle in a foreign country post-retirement

My cousin Amit and his wife Pooja work for the same Fortune 500 company in Sydney, Australia. After a few years of working with MNCs in India, they moved to Australia seven years ago. They recently got their permanent resident (PR) status and have settled down comfortably in Sydney's suburban district known as 'Little India'.

Amit and Pooja are the liveliest people I know. They are full of energy and really know how to work hard and party harder. Married for 15 years now, in their busy corporate lives, they never found time to start a family. And now that both of them are in their forties, they have gotten comfortable with the idea of not having children of their own. In their words, 'It's too much responsibility.'

Both Amit and Pooja had been a little carefree with their finances too. Since they got married, they would often come up to me casually for suggestions on what they should be doing but would always end up procrastinating on financial planning. Then, after many rounds of discussions, they finally started SIPs in three EMFs. After a couple of years, when they started seeing their money add up and compound to larger sums, they also added lump-sum amounts to the same schemes each year when they received their bonuses.

Seven years ago, in 2016, before they were leaving for Sydney, we did a review of their investments. Their total investment value that time had added up to ₹64 lakh and was distributed as follows:

HDFC Flexi-cap Fund = ₹25 lakh
ICICI Prudential Large & Mid Cap Fund = ₹24 lakh
Axis Bluechip Fund = ₹15 lakh

At this time, I had discussed the 1 per cent formula with them to urge them to start thinking about goal-based investing. However, after they moved to Sydney, we didn't have any more conversations on financial guidance.

Due to the increased costs of settling down in a new

country, they couldn't continue investing. Their SIPs stopped, and so did the regular tracking of their existing investments in the MFs. After a couple of years, whatever little savings they could muster quickly went away towards renting bigger and better houses, buying and maintaining cars and in general, towards upgrading their standard of living in their Sydney lifestyle.

As they grew older, they realized that their existing approach to money was not serving them. Their corporate careers had all but exhausted them, and they didn't have anything to show for it in the way of a nest egg. They wanted to take it easy, maybe leave their demanding jobs and do something they both loved to do. Travel was always something they had enjoyed, and they wished they could do that more often. Maybe even make a business out of it. But as it stood, they didn't know if they could afford their lifestyle if even one of them quit their day job. And what would they do after they retire?

As they discussed how they could live a more relaxed life doing what they love, they remembered how I had urged them to adopt the 1 per cent formula. And, in 2023, they got in touch with me to plan out their investments. They told me that they wished to retire to a less stressful lifestyle in the next six years and to pursue other passion areas, especially experiential travel.

We tried to get the hang of the expenses that they would need to plan for post-retirement and arrived at the following (per annum):

Rent = A$30,000
Food and groceries = A$6,000
Maintenance and fuel for two cars (including weekend

drives) = A$5,000
Optional medical insurance = A$3,600
Utilities, including streaming service subscriptions = A$3,600
Eating out (at A$100 a week) = A$5,200
One trip every two years to India = A$2,000
One or two 10-day vacations every year = A$2,500

This totalled up to A$57,900 per year. Subsidies given to them by the Australian government as per their PR status would act as an extra cushion.

In Indian rupees, this worked out to be around ₹32 lakh per annum (or about ₹2.7 lakh a month). This meant that using the 1 per cent formula, we would need to plan for a corpus of ₹2.7 crore.

It was now time to see what they already had. We dug out the details of the old investments and found that the current valuation of the EMFs had jumped from ₹64 lakh to ₹1.62 crore. This was more than two-and-a-half times growth in seven years in a lower-than-average market performance phase. This is where their investments stood in 2023.

HDFC Flexi-cap Fund = ₹67.2 lakh
ICICI Prudential Large & Mid Cap Fund = ₹60.93 lakh
Axis Bluechip Fund = ₹34.2 lakh

This meant we had to contribute another ₹1.08 crore to the corpus. Given they wanted to retire in six years and the need to maintain a three-year cushion, we had to add this ₹1.08 crore in the next three years. We chalked out a plan to restart the SIPs with ₹1 lakh per month (A$1,850). This would help them reach the goal of ₹2.7 crore in the next three years to finally retire after six!

BETTER LATE THAN NEVER: THE RETIRED COUPLE

Objective: Peace of mind and an income to meet their needs

Mrs and Mr Manocha had made one investment in their lives that they were most proud of—their children's education.

Both their children had pursued professional education in medicine and engineering, respectively. Their daughter, Renuka, went on to become a cardiologist, currently working at the Indraprastha Apollo Hospital in Delhi. Their son Apurva, after pursuing computer science at IIT Kanpur, and master's in business administration from IIM Ahmedabad, is now working for a mid-sized IT firm in Pune as its CEO. A common friend had introduced me to Apurva during a family holiday to Goa, and we are now best of friends.

Through Apurva, I met his parents. Both in their 70s, the senior Manochas often reminisce about the simpler times during their career days. Mrs Manocha was a primary-school teacher in one of the most prominent schools in Lucknow, and Mr Manocha was a career public sector undertaking (PSU) banker. Even from their humble salaries, they had managed to fund the education of both children, built their own house in Lucknow and invested in a flat in a housing society in the hills in neighbouring Uttarakhand. Post retirement, they lived on a monthly rental income of ₹12,000 coming from the Uttarakhand flat and returns from an accumulated savings of ₹80 lakh in bank FDs and a few other safe, fixed returns investments.

Unfortunately, this situation didn't create a nice, peaceful retirement they had imagined for themselves. For one, their Uttarakhand flat tenant was making life miserable for them. At that age, they weren't able to deal with his incessant demands and run around to manage the property. The children were too busy in their careers and too far away to take any active role in managing that flat.

While the rent itself was not that lucrative, the Manochas felt they could not let it go because the bank FD rates were going down too. In 2016, FD rates had fallen from 9 per cent a few years back to 7 per cent and were expected to fall further. The monthly income of around ₹60,000 that their ₹80 lakh savings in bank FDs gave them had come down to about ₹47,000. To top that, prices of everything had gone up. They were not able to make ends meet and were too proud, despite multiple offers, to accept financial help from their children.

Finally, Apurva asked me to help them out and organize their investments in a way that they can get a stable, sustainable income.

This was my biggest challenge towards the application of the 1 per cent formula. For someone who had never invested in equity markets and had no experience of the underlying volatility, convincing them of the viability would be a challenge. Of course, there was an easy way out, which was to ask them to stick to the traditional instruments and take help from their children if need be, but I accepted!

My strategy was to make a gradual shift towards EMFs and pick schemes from the less aggressive (hybrid) category of Balanced Advantage Funds. Since they could not afford a long break in their monthly inflows, I had to manipulate the volatility buffer period. So here is what I did.

Instead of the required three years, I put out a waiting period of one year before they could start the withdrawals. To compensate for the balance of the two years of waiting period, I changed the corpus value. I calculated their corpus invested to a value that it would have been two years ago in the same schemes. This would make the situation as if they had invested in the fund two years ago and had one more year to go to complete the volatility buffer period.

For the Manochas, it meant withdrawals of 0.75 per cent from 2017 instead of the 1 per cent they could have withdrawn after a buffer period of three years. That came to about 9 per cent withdrawals every year, a decent percentage compared to the dwindling FD rates.

They first started following the formula strategy in 2016. As we all know, since then the markets have gone through a lot of ups and downs. However, they continued to withdraw 0.75 per cent monthly from the initial corpus value since 2017. The value itself fluctuated and went below principal a few times, which meant long phone calls with Mr Manocha to reiterate the behaviour of the equity markets in the short term and the lucrative long-term prospects of the Indian economy.

Eventually, after the Covid cycle, in 2021, when our markets had made a strong recovery, the corpus had reached more than 30 per cent higher levels even after all the withdrawals since 2017.

Having seen through one major cycle in the markets, the Manochas are now quite comfortable with equity investing. In 2022, they sold off their Uttarakhand flat and put the ₹50 lakh sales proceeds in Flexi-cap EMFs. And again, after a one year waiting period, applying the same manipulation of the volatility buffer to this corpus, they have recently started withdrawing ₹37,500 monthly from this corpus. That is three times more than the amount they were receiving as rent.

And here is how their financial position has shifted:
Monthly income before the 1 per cent formula:

₹47,000 + ₹12,000 = ₹59,000, with an expectation to decrease in future

Monthly income now, after applying the 1 per cent formula:

₹60,000 + ₹37,500 = ₹97,500, with a scope to increase in future

Needless to say, the Manochas are very happy with the way the 1 per cent formula has worked for them and are now very comfortable with their monthly income.

9

A Word of Caution

This book began with a disclaimer, and I would like to bring your attention back to the reality of the stock market—there is no way to guarantee returns. We cannot say with any certainty that a particular portfolio or even the market will give a specific percentage of returns. We can only look at past performances, glean insights from them and create projections of what the future could look like. And given the past few decades of data, the future looks bright indeed—but it isn't a certainty. This is why, when you invest in EMFs, you need to be prepared for market risk. This is why creating the volatility buffer and the emergency fund is so important.

In the 1 per cent formula, I have built three protective layers around your corpus. I have done extensive analysis on different funds and their performance in the last 25 years, and these layers have protected the corpus against market risk in even the worst-performing cases. So, while you secure your financial freedom with the 1 per cent formula, don't forget to add these following layers.

LAYER 1: DIVERSIFICATION

Whoever said don't put all your eggs in one basket was spot on. Diversification is the first step to making your corpus volatility-proof. Spread your corpus across six to 10 schemes across three to five fund houses. Remember, choose your funds and fund managers wisely. Do your research and give your fund manager enough flexibility to tide your corpus over rough patches.

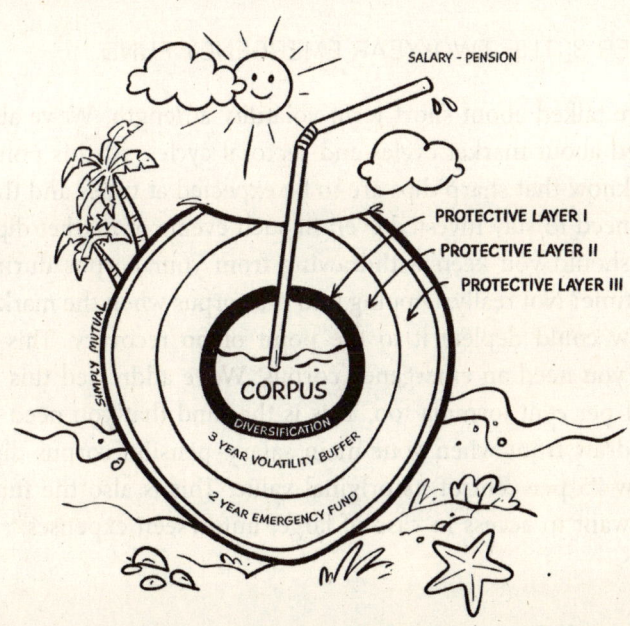

Protect Your Corpus

LAYER 2: THE THREE-YEAR VOLATILITY BUFFER

This is the waiting period in which you let your corpus settle. We talked about this in the chapter on the 1 per cent formula. It is really important that you do not withdraw anything from the corpus in this timeframe and let it adjust to market fluctuations. This waiting period will serve you, especially in case you completed your corpus when the market was at its peak and corrected over the next few years.

LAYER 3: THE TWO-YEAR EMERGENCY FUND

We've talked about short-term volatility at length. We've also talked about market cycles and sectoral cycles. At this point, you know that sharp dips are to be expected at times and that you need to stay invested even in such events of market dips. But should you keep withdrawing from your corpus during this time? Not really. Dipping into the corpus when the market is low could deplete it to the point of no recovery. This is why you need an emergency corpus. We've addressed this in the 1 per cent formula too. This is the fund that you need to withdraw from when your main salary–pension corpus dips below 75 per cent of its original value. This is also the fund you want to access in case of large, unforeseen expenses.

◆

This book has been written after extensive research and analysis. However, past performance can only tell us so much. This is why you need to keep your eyes open and make the right investment choices. Make sure you get a trusted investment professional who can help you actively manage your money.

Even when you start withdrawing funds, a professional can tell you how you can systematically increase your withdrawals over time given your unique needs and the prevailing market conditions. This will ensure that your corpus and your financial freedom is protected.

As you start building your corpus through EMFs, you'll gain more confidence in this approach. You will also get a better sense of how markets operate once you have experienced two to three cycles in the market. That will help you understand that ups and downs are a part of an investor's life. There are many times when markets run ahead of themselves, as proven just before the dot-com bubble burst. They extrapolate high growth in profits and prices go up, only to be corrected in a few years. There are other times when markets run low, like in the aftermath of the 2007–08 financial crisis. But they pick up again as profits continue to soar.

So, invest wisely and go for well-diversified funds managed by experienced fund managers who have shown capability in preserving the value of their funds in the time of crisis.

KEY TAKEAWAYS AND REFLECTIONS

1. To get an understanding of the market, you need to experience two to three cycles of it.
2. Your corpus needs three layers of protection against market cycles:
   a) A diversification layer where you spread the corpus across two to three funds each of three to five fund houses resulting in a portfolio of six to 10 funds in total

b) A cushion of three years to help stabilize against market volatility
c) A two-year emergency fund in a bank FD to tide over any unexpected expenses like medical emergencies

CHEW ON THIS

1. What is the caution you will exercise while investing in EMFs?

10

The 10 Commandments of Wealth Building

'To get rich, you have to be making money while you are asleep.'

—David Bailey

Building wealth isn't really about having a financial degree but rather maintaining a certain attitude and discipline about money. In this book, we've seen how long-term planning and consistent investment can lead to great rewards. In this chapter, I hope to leave you with 10 commandments of wealth building that will serve you in your journey to financial freedom.

1. **Don't save, invest. Invest before you spend.**
   Saving is old school. There was a generation that wanted to keep their money in the bank because it was 'safe'. There was also a generation that put money in earthen pots and buried it in the ground because it was 'safe'.

   Just because they did it doesn't mean you should, too! They probably did not have the facilities or the understanding to make their money work for them. Maybe inflation and cost of living was not such a burden on them. Maybe it was okay to collect the principal and not have it grow for them. Maybe it was a simpler time and a simpler life.

Today, there is so much in the world to explore and experience, and so many opportunities that did not exist earlier. Today, you can be anything, do anything! But you do need resources. And to do what you're passionate about, to experience life, you need to have financial freedom. And that doesn't come from saving—that comes from investing.

Your parents were not wrong in advising you to be cautious about money. It's a good thing to be careful. But it is not in your best interest to be *passive* about it either. By simply working a corporate job and saving your money, you will never get financial freedom. You will never be free of the stress and anxiety of making enough money to meet your needs for a comfortable life. Investing is about being *active* in pursuit of your financial goals.

Most of the 'savings' lose their value over time. The return is so low that after taxes and inflation, there really isn't much that your savings can get you. That's because risk and reward are directly proportional. The less the risk, the lower the reward. So assured returns are very low.

Investing, on the other hand, especially equity investing through MFs, allows you to run a business empire without the headache that comes with it. And as companies in your portfolio grow, your wealth grows too. We already saw how the India growth opportunity is ripe for the taking—there is massive growth projected for the next 30 years! Why not make hay while the sun shines?

In the 1 per cent formula, the volatility buffer creates the safety net for you. And it's in your best interests to understand how it works rather than go for 'safe' instruments.

So, the next time you think of fixed-return investments, think again and invest in EMFs instead!

Equally important is to build the discipline of investing before you spend. Remember the SIPs? Get them going so you can curb wasteful spending.

2. **Think long term, start early, delay gratification**
We talked at length about the only thing that matters in equity markets: investing for the long term. Any genuine financial guru or investor worth their salt will tell you that there is no formula to get rich quick—those are scams. Managing your money is like managing your health. There is no quick fix; you have to give it time and be mindful of it.

Short-term volatility is a market reality, just like long-term growth. The 'traders' that operate in the market will get swayed by the sentiment and cause fluctuations in prices. But these ups and downs correct themselves over a period of time. And it is not even that long a timeframe! We are talking just 15–18 years! So, if you start investing at 27—when, by all assumptions, you have finished your education and started earning—you can retire by 45.

Thinking long term is also about delaying gratification—of not upgrading that car or buying that house. I always advise my clients against buying a house. You are wasting perfectly good money on EMIs. Instead, you can invest that money in EMFs for a few years and actually buy that house, if you really want it, with upfront payment.

In the 1960s, a Stanford professor named Walter Mischel conducted a series of case studies called the 'marshmallow experiment'. He began testing children when they were between four and five years of age and continued the experiment till they grew up. The experiment, in itself, was simple. Each child was settled into a private room. They sat on a chair while a marshmallow was placed on the table in front of them.

At this point, the researcher told the child that they were going to leave the room for a bit and offered a deal to the child. They were told that if they did not eat the marshmallow while the researcher was away, then when the researcher came back, they would get two marshmallows instead. But if the child ate the first one before the researcher came back, then they would not get a second marshmallow.

The choice was simple: one treat right now or two treats later.

The footage was interesting. Some children ate the marshmallow as soon as the researcher left, others tried to not give in to temptation but ultimately gave up and ate it and a few managed to wait the entire time.

As the children grew up, follow-up studies were conducted to track each child's progress in a number of areas. Can you guess the results?

The children who delayed gratification for the second marshmallow performed better in all areas. They had better academic records, lower levels of substance abuse, lower likelihood of obesity, better responses to stress, etc. Even as adults in their 40s, the group that waited for the second marshmallow continued to outperform the others.

The marshmallow experiment proved that the ability to delay gratification is a very important component for becoming successful in life. And the more you can delay gratification, the better your ultimate outcome will be.

That also doesn't mean you sit and wait your entire life to get things that you desire. Like everything in life, managing your money requires a fine balance. Invest enough for tomorrow and spend enough to live comfortably today. Be cautious of unnecessary spending on things that you don't really need, and that actually makes a big difference to when you can actually attain financial freedom.

3. **Keep emotions out of the equation**

We all grow up with some preconceived notions and beliefs about money. In my conversation with Dr Bist, we already established that mindset plays a big role in financial decisions. The psychology of wealth is a major factor in wealth building. In the words of Dr Brad Klontz, a licenced clinical psychologist, 'It is incredibly difficult to go from the middle or working class to become wealthy and the biggest part of that difficulty is psychological.'[1] So much so that it separates the rich from the poor.

We have already seen how operating from the emotions of greed and fear can negatively affect our investment decisions. But what makes us emotionally connected to money is the way we see it as a safety net. What we want in life comes at a cost, and money is most often the way

---

[1] Kinney, Derrick, 'Dr. Brad Klontz - How Your Money Beliefs Are Holding You Back', *Libsyn*, https://tinyurl.com/3856mb62. Accessed on 20 September 2023.

to pay for it. But then, in trying to earn money to pay for what we want to do, money often becomes the hero of the story! If you've found yourself leaning towards that thought process, *stop*. Think again.

The important thing to remember is that money is just a means to an end—it's not an end in itself.

When you are able to take a pragmatic approach towards money, it becomes much easier to manage. You are, then, able to separate facts from feelings. That helps you to avoid being swayed by market sentiment and, instead, keep an eye on company profitability and the overall economic growth of the country—the big picture!

4. **Build financial discipline and stick to it**

Rome was not built in a day, and neither will your wealth. Getting rich requires discipline so deeply ingrained in you that it becomes a habit.

Most of us do not have healthy financial habits. When it comes to money, it is easy to lose track. Impulse buying, unplanned expenses, emergencies—a lot can dent your plans to save. It is also easy to procrastinate, right?

'It's okay if I can't save this month; I'll make up for it next month.'

That 'next month' never comes. And when you can't keep up with the savings plan, it is tempting to just give it up altogether!

On top of that, there is peer pressure. When you see everyone around you buying a fancy car or a house, it becomes important that you do too. At the same time, family members put pressure on you about having your 'own roof over your head'. These factors can derail your financial plans, setting them back considerably.

Building an investing discipline is the most important part of wealth building. Without it, you will probably be lost. Remember, RCA is your friend, and the only way to leverage that is by regular, systematic investing.

A crucial thing to remember about financial discipline is to set *realistic* goals—something that you can achieve consistently without undue stress or discomfort. If you set an SIP amount that is difficult for you to manage every month, you will end up defaulting on it. Better smaller investments than none at all!

The other thing that helps is keeping an eye on the prize. If you have a clear image in your mind of what you are investing for, it motivates you to keep going. So, don't lose sight of your goal, and the journey will become that much easier.

5. **Beware of market tips**
Equity markets are full of people who will offer you tips on stocks that could mean a big win. The only way you'll win with that is by ignoring them. When you act on market tips, you are gambling—and we've seen how that doesn't really contribute to your wealth.

Market tips are speculations at best, and no one can predict with any certainty whether they will come true. Many people have lost their life savings chasing after these tips and trying to make a quick buck.

Often, tips are tinged with market sentiment as well. When things are going great, everyone tells you to invest. But when markets tank, the usual hue and cry is to get out while you can. As an advisor with 25 years in the industry, I can tell you that this is not always the right call to take. In fact, you should be staying invested, if not investing more, when the markets are down! Be optimistic, especially when others are fearful. On the other hand, never invest a lump-sum amount when the market is at its peak, and everyone is excited about it.

Equity markets offer a great opportunity to build wealth, but only to those who approach it with the right mindset. Stop trying to time the markets or capitalize on tips. Instead, use SIPs that are one of the best ways to make use of this opportunity.

6. **Find the right fund and the right advisors**

 How you invest is important, and where you invest is equally important. We talked about the various types of MFs that are available in the market today, and some of them may seem more lucrative than others. However, as an individual investor, your best bet is investing in flexi-cap or multi-cap funds that are sector agnostic. Try and pick the ones that are managed by an experienced team that has managed three to four market cycles. And finally, choose the right investment advisor who can guide you through the process and help you stay the course in times of indecision.

7. **Know your money**

 The success of financial planning depends on your understanding of your money and how it delivers returns as also your willingness to understand it!

 For example, I have spent a lot of time trying to persuade prospective clients against investing in unit linked insurance plans (ULIPs). Every financial advisor understands that one should always keep insurance and investments separate. But many of them still sell ULIPs to their clients because they get more commission. And people buy it even when returns are low! Why? Because they are unable to grasp the concept and purpose of insurance.

In ULIPs, you see some amount of money coming back to you, and so the outcome becomes tangible. On the other hand, when you buy term-insurance, there is no money back. So, it feels like a waste of money. What people fail to understand is that insurance is a protection against risk. The insurer is charging you money so that if something goes wrong, you get many times the amount that you have paid for it. If nothing goes wrong, that's good, right?

Unit linked insurance plans, on the other hand, mix insurance with investment. This is why you usually pay a higher premium for them than your term-insurance. They still keep an amount aside to factor in the cost of insurance, and the remaining amount gets invested in something like an MF—this is what comes back to you as money. So, you've essentially still paid the cost of term-insurance without any returns and, in addition, paid a massive agent commission (sometimes, as much as 30 per cent) from your pocket!

There is a lot more to financial instruments than meets the eye, and, therefore, you need to keep an eye on where your money is going, how it is being used and what are the returns you are getting.

Again, some advisors may inflate the returns when suggesting an investment avenue. You should always look at a post-tax and post-inflation return to make comparisons between options.

8. Don't panic! Stay invested

Does India have a great growth story? Yes.
Do you stand to benefit from it? Yes.
Can things go wrong? Yes.

We've seen how markets are volatile in the short term. Sometimes they are way ahead of the profits (peak) and, at other times, they trail profits. If you have the misfortune of investing when the market is at its peak, you may find yourself losing a fair bit of money when it corrects again. There could also be a market crash due to events like a pandemic that could cause a sharp drop.

And that's where most people panic. It is a very understandable response to watching a big chunk of your money being wiped out. But this is where you need an objective look at the crash. Don't look at it in absolute terms, but in percentages. For example, if you lost ₹10 lakh in a market crash—that seems like a big amount, right? But what if your corpus itself was ₹1 crore? Then it is just 10 per cent of the value. If your corpus was ₹4 crore, in this crash, you might lose ₹40 lakh—but that's still only 10 per cent of your portfolio. So, the bigger the portfolio, the bigger the loss seems in absolute terms—triggering panic.

Does that mean your money is lost forever? No, not if you stay invested.

In the long term, markets will recover and you will end up multiplying your money. The bigger problem is not even markets crashing but that they stay flat for four to five years. That could mean that you might have to eat into your corpus, leaving it depleted enough to not recover. That is what the three-year volatility buffer and the two-year emergency fund in the 1 per cent formula protect you from.

But these short-term shocks can put a dent in anyone's plans. This is why, as a rule, you should avoid lump-sum withdrawals. It allows your corpus to recover from short-term volatility.

9. **Have a cushion, be vigilant**
When your corpus reaches a value that you had planned for all along, it could be tempting to give in and start withdrawing from it immediately.

But wait.

That three-year volatility buffer that we have built into the process is important. It allows your corpus to settle down and become more resilient to market changes. It also protects against events where you finished your corpus building when the markets were at their peak. In that event, the value will fall over the next few years as markets correct. The three-year waiting period before withdrawals allows your funds to absorb these shocks. Equally important is the emergency corpus worth two years of your expenses.

But just having a cushion does not mean you stop keeping an eye on your money. *The idea of the 1 per cent formula is financial freedom, not financial negligence.*

In case of an unforeseen market event that severely impacts the value of your corpus, you need to be cognizant of that. You have to give your corpus the leeway to build back. And so, in those times, when the value drops below 25 per cent of the principal value, stop withdrawing 1 per cent from this corpus and move to the emergency fund instead.

10. Get into the 1 per cent mindset

The 1 per cent formula is not just a way of investing; it is also a mindset. It's about delaying gratification, so you don't erode all your wealth in chasing after things you don't really need. At the same time, it's about living a life of comfort and wellbeing. It's about leaving the financial beliefs of past generations in the past and creating new goals for yourself and the life you want to live. It's about evaluating major decisions and their financial implications, not just on today but on your future as well. It's about looking at everything from the 1 per cent mindset.

Let us take the most common big purchase people make—a house, sometimes even two. Buying a house when you are younger burdens you with massive EMIs. No amount of rent or appreciation will be able to support your future needs. If you are able to hold off on buying a house for a few years, that EMI can actually build a substantial corpus for you—enough that you can use the 1 per cent withdrawals to take any similar house you fancy on rent. Or, if you are really keen on buying it, you can do that while leaving a significant portion of the corpus to grow.

My friends were keen to jointly own a vacation home in Goa. Whenever we would evaluate the option, I would point out the opportunity cost with the 1 per cent formula. Instead of buying that ₹1.5 crore apartment that we may use for only three months in a year, we could rent a different one every time at ₹1.5 lakh per month without blocking that lump-sum investment. Imagine! In a year, we could have an ₹18 lakh vacation budget. That gives us so much choice! We could rent a villa for one vacation, five-star hotel rooms for another or a quaint luxury cottage if we feel like it. Why buy when you can rent!

A Letter to the Individual Investor

Thank you for staying with me on this journey. I hope this book has given you insights into the world of investing and how just a little more discipline and attention to detail could help you attain your financial freedom.

When I started writing this book, I wanted to simplify investing for you. I wanted to help you shake some of your deep-rooted investing mind blocks and financial beliefs. I wanted to give you some food for thought on how to best use your money and plan for your dreams. I hope I have been successful in this endeavour. Nothing would please me more if, as a reader, you decide to take control of your financial journey and re-look at the way you have been managing your money.

I have personally been able to achieve financial independence by investing in equities and my thought process today makes me spot opportunities in every situation. Getting stuck in city traffic makes me think of so many new cars being bought, giving me the sense that my MF NAV is rising. Congestion at airports = new terminals under-construction = NAV rising. So many home-deliveries happening = rising affordability = rising employment = NAV rising. Smooth multi-lane highways with FASTag toll gates = NAV rising.

It is a dream that my readers would share my enthusiasm about the India growth story, get into the mode of seeing India's progress in every aspect of life and understand how we can all participate in this progress by investing in equities via MFs.

A young, hard-working, future-ready India is creating this opportunity for us for the next 30 years.

Well, you know what to do now! Go out there and get cracking towards your financial freedom.

I wish you the wealth of time!

Acknowledgements

Writing this book has been a rewarding experience. I would have missed out on this if not for the people who stood with me and encouraged me to take this step.

First and foremost, I would like to thank my mentor and guide Prashant Jain. His clarity of thought and simplicity has been a constant source of inspiration for me in my career, my personal life and in writing this book.

I went through many moments of indecision on what I wrote. I thank my wife Sindhuja for her tremendous patience in reading and re-reading my drafts and her invaluable opinions that helped move this book forward.

I am deeply thankful to my friends Supriya Jain and Dr Anuranjan Bist for contributing their valuable expertise to the book.

I am also thankful to my friends Rahul Koul and Gaurav Sood, who convinced me that business and friendship can go together. They planted the idea of SimplyMutual and encouraged me to take the leap; to my clients, friends and family, who placed their trust in me to manage their hard-earned money.

I am indebted to my friends Ashutosh Pant, Kamaljeet Singh, Vikrant Jairath, Rishikesh Sunke, Pankaj Singh and Sushil Nifadkar for their support and invaluable contributions in making this book a reality.

Last but not least, I would like to thank all my colleagues in the mutual fund industry, who supported my humongous data-mining exercise.